INDEMNITY STATEMENT

An appropriate citation for this magazine is:
The KPI Institute, Performance Magazine, no. 1, September, 2015, Melbourne, Australia

Published by:

THE KPI INSTITUTE

The KPI Institute
Life.lab Building
198 Harbour Esplanade, Suite 606
Melbourne Docklands, VIC 3008, Australia

Telephone
Headquarters: +61 3 9028 2223
Middle East Division: +971 4 311 6556
European Division: +40 3 6942 6935
South East Asia Division: +60 3 2742 1357

E-mail: office@kpiinstitute.org

www.kpiinstitute.org

CONTENTS

PORTRAIT   **22**

INTERVIEWS   **11**

AROUND THE WORLD   **26**

STAFF

EDITORIAL COORDINATION

Aurel Brudan
CEO, The KPI Institute
Adrian Brudan
General Manager TKI – EMEA
Adelina Chelniciuc
Head of Publishing & Media
Diana Zărnescu
Senior Editor & Publisher
Denisa Călin
Senior Editor & Publisher

EDITORIAL TEAM

Cristina Tărâță
Head of Research Programs
Andreea Vecerdea
Head of Strategy and Performance
Oana Gavril
Project Manager for SE Asia Region
Mihai Toma
Head of Professional Practice
TKI MENA
Mihai Păculea
Head of Digital Marketing
Andrada-Iulia Ghețe
Head of Innovation
Paul Albu
Senior Business Research Specialist
Marcela Presecan
Business Research Specialist
Ramona Gligorea
Talent Development Specialist

GUEST WRITERS

Manuel Hila
Maria Desmons-Macrea

DESIGN

Design coordination
Daniela Fajardo
Senior Graphic Design Specialist

Design team
Javier Rocha
Head of Graphic Design

EDITOR'S NOTE

After more than one year of resounding success, the time has come for PERFORMANCE Magazine to move closer to the professional readership by integrating the best content published online, alongside exclusive materials, into its printed counterpart.

Encompassing The KPI Institute's experience and research, PERFORMANCE Magazine – Printed Edition will provide its readership with first-hand how-to, resources and insights from practice, so as to assist them in their performance endeavors and in becoming state-of-the art professionals.

Shipped directly to you, this quarterly publication embeds exhaustive analysis on various topics related to performance management, by offering expert interviews, extensive research studies, concept presentations, insights from practice, alongside software or hardware reviews, and educational resources recommendations.

The accelerated evolution of performance-related practices and tools, together with their utility in multiple functional areas and industries, have influenced us to expand our areas of expertise, along with our portfolio of services. Now, PERFORMANCE Magazine offers exclusive access to an excerpt of our expertise and research, through well-documented, yet easy-to-read articles on a large range of topics.

Featured in every edition, there will be interviews with renowned experts in the field of performance management, compliments of our editorial team's participation in multiple performance-related events all around the world. An extra feature is that each issue includes details about one preeminent expert in the field, pointing to their performance initiatives in both personal lives, and professional endeavors.

Gain insights into public sector implementation processes from various countries and nations, as each edition will feature extensive analyses on the subject, documented by our Business Research Specialists. Also, best practices, alongside the latest trends, will be offered for a wide variety of performance-related sub-domains, from Strategy to KPIs and from Customer Service to Innovation performance.

Not least, the magazine will feature recommended resources for professionals interested in combining leisure and professional development, such as books and documentaries.

We are always interested in gaining insights from practitioners activating in the performance management field. If you are interested in becoming a Guest Editor, or having your interview featured in our magazine.contact us at: **performance@kpiinstitute.org**

Get inspired by discovering successful performance endeavors, combine leisure with highly useful, educational reading, gain a performance-oriented approach to both organizational and personal life and stay up-to-date with the latest developments in the field, now both in online and in print!

Adelina Chelniciuc.
Head of Publishing & Media.
The KPI Institute

CERTIFICATION PROGRAMS 2015

C-PP
- ▶ Personal Performance Framework
- ▶ Self-improvement
- ▶ Lifelogging

C-SBP
- ▶ Context Analysis Techniques
- ▶ Strategy Formulation
- ▶ Business Planning

C-CSP
- ▶ Customer Service Strategy
- ▶ Customer Satisfaction Enablers
- ▶ Customer Advocacy

C-EPM
- ▶ Individual KPIs
- ▶ Competencies
- ▶ Behaviors

C-KPI
- ▶ KPI Selection
- ▶ KPI Documentation
- ▶ Target Setting

C-B
- ▶ Benchmarking Process
- ▶ Benchmarking Techniques
- ▶ Data Comparison

C-SP
- ▶ Supplier Contract Management and SLAs
- ▶ Supplier Relationship Management
- ▶ Supplier Performance Monitoring and Reporting

CERTIFIED STRATEGY AND PERFORMANCE MANAGEMENT PROFESSIONAL

Awarded to professionals holding all 4 core certifications: C-SBP, C-KPI, C-PI and C-EPM

C-PI
- ▶ Reporting
- ▶ Decision Making
- ▶ Initiative Management

C-DA
- ▶ Data Validity
- ▶ Analysis Techniques
- ▶ Performance Index

C-DV
- ▶ Content Standardization
- ▶ Channels Selection
- ▶ SFERA Framework

Other connected certifications

Certified Personal Performance Professional
Certified Strategy and Business Planning Professional
Certified Customer Service Performance Professional
Certified Employee Performance Management Professional
Certified KPI Professional
Certified Benchmarking Professional
Certified Supplier Performance Professional
Certified Data Analysis Professional
Certified Performance Improvement Professional
Certified Data Visualization Professional

Scheduled Courses in 2015

CERTIFICATION TRAINING COURSES IN 25 COUNTRIES

Africa	Americas	Asia Pacific	Europe	Middle East
Morocco	Brazil	Australia	Austria	Bahrain
Nigeria	Canada	China	Romania	Egypt
South Africa	Mexico	India	UK	Kuwait
	USA	Indonesia		Oman
		Malaysia		Qatar
		Singapore		Saudi Arabia
		Thailand		Turkey
				UAE

ORGANIZATION
- **2004** Year of establishment
- **25** # Certified trainers
- **4** # Offices around the globe. Australia, Malaysia, Romania, UAE

RESEARCH
- **28,000** # Organizations assisted through smartKPIs.com
- **20,475** # KPI examples published on smartKPIs.com
- **11** # Years spent on researching performance best practice

EDUCATION
- **3,400** # Professionals trained
- **614** # Client organizations
- **554** # Training days delivered
- **228** # Education programs delivered
- **115** # Open training courses delivered
- **113** # In-house training courses delivered

For more details: **store.kpiinstitute.org**

THE KPI INSTITUTE'S PROFESSIONAL CERTIFICATION PROGRAMS

To browse through our upcoming training courses and select the solution that best addresses your personal and professional objectives we recommend you visit: **http://store.kpiinstitute.org/scheduled-courses**

Certified Strategy and Business Planning Professional

The course will help improve the business planning process and long-term organizational performance, through the use of strategic planning tools that will ultimately lead to smarter and quicker strategic decisions.

Certified KPI Professional

This program is meant to improve the practical skills in working with KPIs and developing instruments like scorecards and dashboards. Participants will acquire a sound framework to measure KPIs, starting from the moment they are selected, until results are collected in performance reports.

Certified Performance Improvement Professional

This course offers insights and best practices for improving performance in different scenarios, from data analysis and reporting, decision making and initiative management, to building a performance culture.

Certified Employee Performance Management Professional

Attendees will gain exposure to best practices and key concepts and will learn how to establish and use criteria for performance evaluations, from implementation to improvement and maintenance of the company's employee performance management system.

Certified Personal Performance Professional

The two-day interactive program will help you understand personal performance, by explaining the benefits and clarifying the process of measuring it. It focuses on identifying ways to boost your performance outside working hours.

Certified Data Visualization Professional

An exclusive framework that provides insights on effective visual communication, through a rigorous approach to creating visual representations of vast information, techniques of standardization and tailored data visualization tools.

Certified Data Analysis Professional

Attendants will understand through practical learning how to effectively collect, analyze and interpret data by enabling managers/analysts to draw insights from both quantitative and qualitative data, based on historical statistics and trend analysis.

Certified Benchmarking Professional

Benchmarking methodological uniqueness is represented by the identification and analysis of the processes that lead to a superior performance of a company, offering the opportunity to compare an organization's performance against industry competitors.

Certified Supplier Performance Professional

Participants' skills in managing supplier performance and developing a strategic approach to procurement will be developed by enabling the identification of performance gaps and implementing action agreements with suppliers.

Certified Customer Service Performance Professional

Participants will not only understand the importance and implementation phases for the Customer Service Excellence standards, but they will also be given the necessary tools to implement it internally and measure its impact externally.

> No objective to work towards? Over 40% of employees say so

Recent findings shared by the CIPD Employee Outlook tracker pointed out that 44% of employees do not relate to their organization's objectives and do not feel that they work towards achieving a specific goal or objective. The other 56%, however, said that, by having an objective, their performance at work increases and might help them advance in their careers.

The results of this bi-annual report also show that employees' preferences revolve around performance feedback, more specifically individual feedback offered more frequently than once a year.

CIPD's Employee Outlook report compiles the responses of 2,226 employees from various industries and organizations to extract views upon the places they work for, their colleagues and superiors, as well as upon the performance management systems implemented.

> Australia's Olympic team might get a touch of measurement for Rio 2016

Researchers from the **University of South Australia** have recently developed a system that should monitor the athletes' heart rate, in order to determine how well they recover from training. This technology could be used for the Australian representative team at the 2016 Summer Olympics from Rio de Janeiro, according to ABC Online.

This also becomes a good risk assessment tool as, by indicating the athletes who have not properly recovered from training, it can prevent injuries. Also, as Professor Jon Buckley, director of the Alliance for Research in Exercise, Nutrition and Activity at the University of South Australia declared for ABC Online, being able to measure the players' rate of recovery could help in implementing a customized training regime, in improving the team performance and the game strategy.

The system, patented by University of South Australia, is developed in collaboration with the South Australian Sports Institute and a Finnish heart rate monitor company.

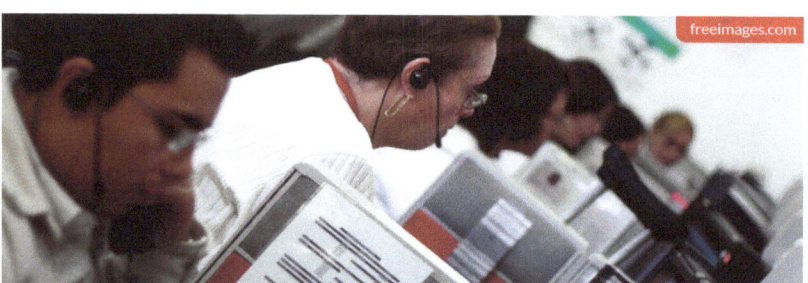
freeimages.com

> The Customer Experience Management Market will grow with roughly $ 5 billion by 2019

Customer Experience Management (CEM) is becoming very popular, due to the analytical tools used to process and analyze customer feedback, and more and more companies have started investing in such solutions, according to the market research company MarketsandMarkets.

As stated in their report, "Customer Experience Management Market (VOC Analytics, Feedback Management, Web Analytics, Text Analytics, Speech Analytics) - Advanced Technologies, Touch Points, Adoption Trends, Market Size & Forecasts (2014 – 2019)", the industry is forecasted to grow from $3.77 billion in 2014 to $8.39 billion in 2019.

CEM is an aggregation of processes, based on a wide variety of technologies that aim at gathering customer feedback, understanding their expectations and improving the overall customer experience through different touch points.

Another segment of the market report details Customer Relationship Management (CRM) as the strategy of managing and nurturing a company's interactions with its clients. The CRM application manages sales activities, marketing and customer services by using data management, business intelligence and analytical tools.

> Improving patient care by reporting performance

More and more hospitals include performance data on publicly reported measures into their annual goals, as stated by **Infection Control Today (ICT)**.

According to ICT, public reporting programs are a part of a strategy that the Centers for Medicare & Medicaid Services (CMS) implemented in order to improve outcomes for hospitalized patients and to encourage improvement efforts.

70% of the assessed hospitals agreed that "public reporting stimulates the quality improvement activity" in terms of mortality, readmission, process and patient experience measures, according to ICT. However, as stated by the same source, 45.7% to 58.6% percent of hospital leaders were concerned that focusing on publicly reported quality measures could lead to neglecting the other important topics. Another common concern is that hospital employees would adopt a negative behavior in order to show improvement instead of actually taking measures.

> Preventing illegal cyber gambling with KPIs in Kuala Lumpur

All chief district police officers (**OCPD**) are likely to implement a Key Performance Indicator (KPI) to measure the effectiveness of their measures for fighting illegal cyber gambling, as the Home Minister Dato' Seri Dr. Ahmad Zahid Hamidi recently declared for the Malaysian newspaper The Star Online.

The introduction of such a KPI is part of the measures taken in order to deal with this problem, which affects the entire nation, along with initiatives such as a tactical squad of 200 officers that, starting from December, will conduct raids in order to prevent illegal cyber gambling. Also, 53 online gambling websites were identified and blocked.

OCPDs are not the only Malaysian public organization that will be assessed by using KPIs until the end of this year. According to The Star Online, the political party Umno will also be evaluated, in terms of progress, by using KPIs at both divisional and branch level.

> To what extent are US governmental agencies using performance data today?

The use of performance information for various management activities and decision making in US agencies has decreased over the last few years, according to a recently released report, compiled by the **Government Accountability Office**.

In order to evaluate the implementation of the GPRA Modernization Act of 2010, GAO compiled an index derived from a set of questions, extracted from the most recent surveys (2007 and 2013) and used statistical analysis to identify practices that are significantly related to the use of the performance information index.

According to GAO, government-wide, the use of performance data has decreased in the period 2007-2013. Out of the 24 assessed entities, 6 have experienced statistically significant changes. Only 2 agencies have shown a significantly increasing trend (the Office of Personnel Management and the Department of Labor), while within agencies such as the Department of Veterans Affairs, the National Aeronautics and Space Administration, the Department of Energy and the Nuclear Regulatory Commission, the use of performance data has significantly decreased throughout the last 6 years.

Another important finding was the connection between the use of performance information and engagement: the agencies whose managers reported a great engagement in these practices have also experienced increases in terms of using performance information.

> New risk management guidelines for APIA

The Australian Pipeline Industry Association (APIA) has recently developed an increased focus in understanding and managing the impacts of fatigue on employees' physical and cognitive performance.

The risks that fatigue presents to the pipeline industry were compiled by APIA in their "Fatigue Risk Management Guidelines". Through these Guidelines, APIA encourages members to implement Fatigue Risk Management Systems (FRMS), which should include a systematic approach to risk management, training for workers, as well as policies and procedures to support the fatigue management strategy.

According to APIA's guidelines, a FRMS should contain: a fatigue risk management policy, hours of work monitoring, fatigue risk management processes, fatigue management training and education for employees, management and families, a fatigue reporting system for employees, sleep disorder management, fatigue incident investigation, as well as internal and external auditing and safety assurance processes.

APIA is the peak body representing Australasia's pipeline infrastructure, with a focus on gas transmission.

> Qlik's new Business Intelligence tool

Qlik has recently launched its first device-independent, self-service visualization tool, which allows users to create customized data analyses in order to have an instant overview of the results and connections that appear.

Qlik Sense is an intuitive analytics tool that enables the generation of personalized reports and dynamic dashboards to explore vast amounts of data.

Relationships between data dimensions are presented in Smart Visualizations and can be discovered by using the Smart Search function. Qlik Sense also allows the creation of visualizations through a user friendly drag-and-drop function.

PERFORMANCE IMPROVEMENT
AND KPIS FORUM

SEPTEMBER 9th - 11th, 2015 • HOTEL JW MARRIOTT • KUALA LUMPUR

60+ participants

14+ keynote presentation and panel discussions

12+ speakers and panelists

3 days

1 report launch

The first week of the fall season brought forth the Performance Improvement and KPIs Forum which took place between September 9th and 11th, in Kuala Lumpur, Malaysia.

What makes this event special is that it represents the first of its kind to be organized within the Asia Pacific region, with a special focus centered on cutting-edge solutions for business improvement.

Regional thought leaders teamed-up with international business experts to share, teach and learn the new directions of the contemporary organizational world, alongside the most appropriate tools and processes that allow experts to manage and improve the corporate dimensions.

The 3 days of the event were built upon 3 main activity pillars:

Keynote presentations
where leaders in their domain revealed best practices, as they have come to regards them;

Successful case studies
where experts detailed on the specific phases of implementing functional performance measurement systems;

Networking sessions and panel discussions
where interaction and sharing were the main mediums for gathering information about strategy implementations and reviewing.

The most extensive part of the event consisted in the presentations delivered by over a dozen speakers, each of them experts and leaders in their respective business domains.

EVENTS

The first Asia Pacific Forum dedicated to promoting cutting edge solutions for your business improvement!

The majority of keynote speakers live and work in Malaysia, and can thus be considered as accustomed to the culture and business environment specific to the ASEAN professional world.

From Human Resources specialists, such as **Shazmi Ali**, to Talent and Organizational Development experts represented by **Mei Lynn Chan**, **Monir Azzouzi**, or **Wan Erzin Sazli**, to Productivity & Quality Management leaders like **Abdul Wahab Hassan** and Chief Financial Officers such as **Haris Aziz** and **Aiza Azreen**, who is the Chief Strategy and Transformation Officer at a leading Malaysian bank, all brought forth valuable insights from within their practice domains, openly sharing experiences that peers can use to enhance their knowledge and expertise.

An outer-regional perspective was brought by speakers who came to the Performance Improvement and KPIs Forum from as far as Australia namely, **David Vandervlist**, the Assistant Director of Strategic Planning, from the United Arab Emirates, represented by the Managing Director of The KPI Institute in the region, **Teodora Gorski**, two preeminent Human Resources and Talent Development specialists, who both came from Singapore: **May-Lene Tan**, HR Head, and **Caroline Palmstedt**, Regional Talent Development Lead and, last but not least, The KPI Institute's own CEO, **Aurel Brudan**.

The topics tackled within the three-day conference all sought business improvement practices. Thus, from KPI selection, Balanced Scorecard System, analytics and KPI software, to less technical topics such as talent development, organizational effectiveness and maintaining increased performance levels, all were comprised in multiple presentations that ensured a full palette of business improvement solutions for all participants present at the event.

The two workshops scheduled for the

last day of the event engaged participants in the selections and target setting process for KPIs and in the activity of aligning and building a performance-oriented culture as two essential phases of Performance Improvement.

Included in between the presentations, several special events diversified the event's procedures with panel discussions on the essentials of being a high performer, the importance of alignment, both discussions being complemented by the launch of the Performance Improvement in ASEAN 2015 report.

Thus, 3 days dedicated to performance improvement have ended swiftly, but not without results as all participants admitted to the benefits of having and maintaining a constant contact with a panel of same-minded specialists, environment that only events of this kind can offer.

FIVE STEPS TO BUILDING A SUSTAINABLE PERFORMANCE CULTURE
Engage. Stimulate. Train. Reward. Energize.

■ **CRISTINA TĂRÂȚĂ**

These five key words represent some valuable drivers that, if correctly and constantly implemented, can help you build an organizational culture oriented towards performance. Give it time and thought and, eventually, this endeavor will provide a productive and positive working environment.

> **Engage** your employees! Engagement is reflected in the discretionary effort an employee is willing to put into his work. This goes beyond the feeling of satisfaction and motivation, and research has shown it yields a significant impact on productivity, employee turnover and customer satisfaction. Engagement happens when employees clearly understand what is expected from them and how success looks like, when they are given the tools to do their job right, when they have a certain degree of autonomy and when they trust and respect the organization's purpose and leadership.

> **Stimulate** employees, by using gamification – the inclusion of game elements into the working environment. By designing all sorts of contests between departments and teams, employees are motivated to perform better, to "win the game". Competitiveness is part of human nature and, if adequately coordinated, it can bring forth the best in people.

> **Train** your staff, therefore provide them with the instruments they need to improve their competencies. After you have set clear performance expectations, you must ensure that your staff has opportunities to learn, grow and become better employees, and training is a good tool for addressing these needs. It also shows employees that they are being supported in order to achieve their objectives.

> **"Reward"** performance! It is not enough to measure the progress, you must take actions and reward good results. Rewards do not necessarily have to be financial bonuses, they can also consist of nonfinancial nudges, such as tickets to the movies, a golden star, a celebration with colleagues. Rewarding should not take place only when you conduct performance evaluations, but also each time someone does something good, and it can be as simple as an acknowledgement of their achievement.

> **Energize**, by constantly activating all of the above elements and understanding that these are not one time events, but rather a never ending cycle.

Influencing or changing the organizational culture is not easy and the outcomes are not immediate. On the contrary, benefits become palpable in the long run. The entire purpose of building a performance culture is to ensure employees are more productive, more creative and more dedicated to their jobs and to the organization.

Alan Thomson

Managing Director Abu Dhabi Sewerage Services Company

André de Waal

Associate Professor of Strategic Management at the Maastricht School of Management

Rahul Deo Gupta

Corporate Head of Strategy, Planning, Operational Excellence, Abunayyan

Tor Bøe-Lillegraven

Head of CCI Business, Consulting

Rick Edgeman

Professor of Sustainability & Enterprise Performance, ICOA, Aarhus University

INTERVIEWS

Performance management means doing the job you do, but doing it better. It means exploring and understanding the processes that you follow, walking through the processes, even re-engineering them and then evaluating where you have gone with your exercise, if you have improved your performance through measurement.

Alan Thomson

Managing Director
Abu Dhabi Sewerage Services
Company, UAE

Being present at the 2014 edition of the Strategy Leaders Forum, held in Dubai, the PERFORMANCE Magazine team was privy to valuable insights on the latest thoughts and trends in strategy formulation and execution, organizational performance and business excellence.

Our correspondent, present at the event, caught up with Alan Thomson, the Managing Director at the Abu Dhabi Sewerage Services Company. In his interview, he discussed the link between strategic planning and performance management, the recent improvements he has observed in the field and some handy, experience based ways of overcoming performance management challenges and establishing a performance oriented corporate culture.

1. What does the term Performance Management mean to you?

Performance management means doing the job you do, but doing it better. It means exploring and understanding the processes that you follow, walking through the processes, even re-engineering them and then evaluating where you have gone with your exercise, if you have improved your performance through measurement. The measures have to reflect very closely what your business focuses on. But basically, it is about doing the job you do, but doing it better.

2. What is the relation between Strategic Planning and Performance Management?

The relation is very close. Performance management has to have a plan in order to help you improve. If you don't know, if you don't understand what you are doing, then it is very difficult to know if you have improved or if you have gone back. By implementing a strategic plan, you have a better understanding of what your objectives are. Strategic planning will guide you and provide a framework for you to improve your work, your business and your service delivery.

3. How do you see the disciplines of strategy and PM in your geographical area today?

I work in the Middle East and I would say it is improving. There is much more awareness now. Nine years ago, people didn't recognize that we had customers. They were consumers or users, now we have customers. And this is a big step, although it sounds small. Now, we are aware that people should value your services, so the services should be good and according to their expectations. The Abu Dhabi government is very constructive and supportive in pushing good strategic management and performance through the government industries, and we are one of these utilities which is essential for the growth of UAE, and this had been recognized by the government and supported not only in terms of their reactions and governmental administrative support, but also with financial support.

4. Which are the main challenges organizations face in developing strategy and managing performance?

One of the main challenges is the change of directions, so external or third parties, such as government, new legislations which impact very dramatically on the work that we do. So, in order to manage ourselves well we have to build flexibility, and this flexibility enables us to review quickly what we are doing, with the support of government agencies, and to appropriately redirect what we need to do to accommodate the new legislation or the changes the government imposes. The link between government and businesses is very short in Abu Dhabi. Something that is decided in the government circle quickly impacts on businesses, so we have to be very aware of the political situation, both with small and large "p", so both government and people related politics, and we have to understand what the government's priorities are, and that they can change, because the world is a changing place. I think the main challenge is the external change, and how to integrate that into your strategy so that your strategy doesn't go in one direction, when the government wants you to go in other direction.

5. What advice would you give to practitioners working in this field, for overcoming these challenges?

I would say don't have anything fixed forever! You have to look, listen and be very attentive to the changes that happen. By doing that you can embrace the changes, understand what the directions are and alter the direction of your business to help deliver what the government is looking for. So my advice is always don't be too strict about your strategy, because it can change and it will change.

6. Which were the recent achievements in generating value from performance management in your organization?

We have got a program management exercise, a program management office which we put in place to deliver a strategic investment over our business, and that

You have to think, first of all, what this will bring to the organization, what is the added value, and if you decide it is very important, then do it and stick with it, because if you don't stick with it, performance management will not give you its true benefits.

has been a big success. We branded it, and the brand traveled across the globe. It has been highly successful, very well-known and noticed by all the involved parties, the stakeholders, government – we had visits from senior government people to help the launch of this program – this has increased the awareness on the importance and utility, on why is it important for Abu Dhabi's growth to have this kind of services in place, and this all has been done through strategic planning: the evaluation of where we are and where we need to be and how we can close the gap between the starting point and where we need to be with Abu Dhabi's growth and development over the next 25-30 years.

7. What would you recommend as an approach for building a performance oriented culture?
I think you have to engage your colleagues. You need the buy-in from everybody that is working with you, they cannot see it as extra work. As busy as they are, they might think that another initiative will be a burden or more work load. So you have to get them engaged and help them recognize that this will help them deliver their work rather than stop them from moving forward. We do that by good communication. We use multiple forms of communication, whether it is our website, email, meetings, word of mouth, messages on our text system, and of course formal meetings to launch and review strategies on an annual or bi-annual basis. By doing that, we get the employees engaged. But we also have to get stakeholders engaged and we have an exercise when we go to our stakeholders, have interviews or meetings with them and try to understand what their frustrations are. By listening to them, we can hopefully improve our internal processes.

André de Waal
Associate Professor of Strategic Management at the Maastricht School of Management, Netherlands

During the 2014 PMA Conference, held in Aarhus, Denmark, our editors were able to access valuable insights from some of the most highly skilled and experienced academics and practitioners in the field of Performance Management.

Here, the PERFORMANCE Magazine team got the opportunity to connect with André de Waal, Associate Professor of Strategic Management at the Maastricht School of Management (Netherlands) and get his insights on the current state of the performance management field and his thoughts on the future of the discipline.

1. Which are the main challenges that organizations face today in implementing Performance Management systems?
The main challenge is discipline, when companies decide to actually do performance management. If you talk to both top and middle management, what you hear is that their agendas are full, they have so much on their plate and this is not a thing they need to do. You have to think, first of all, what this will bring to the organization, what is the added value, and if you decide it is very important, then do it and stick with it, because if you don't stick with it, performance management will not give you its true benefits.

2. What are the 2014 key trends in Performance Management?
In this conference, I have heard a lot about sustainability. I am not sure if this is a key trend. I think a very clear trend is represented by High Performance Organizations, which involve sustainability, but it is the sustainability of performance, which is something else. What organizations are dealing with is getting out of the recession, regaining and surpassing their performance, getting on a high level and staying there. This means that a second trend is motivating people in this new era of social media. How do you keep them interested? Can you do this with the rigid performance management system or you have to find a more flexible way?

3. If you are to give three pieces of advice to companies on how to manage their performance, what would they be?
The first one would be to create a big picture. Create a vision of what your company could be. And here I come back to High Performance Organizations, because everyone wants to achieve high performance. But what does it actually mean? Paint me a picture, let's say for 3-5 years from now, how will your company look like? Only then you can start thinking what your role should be in there and how performance management can help you create this High Performance Organization. The interesting thing, and this goes back to your previous question, is that this becomes inspiration, because people will say "Why do I need to use performance management?", but then they realize "Wait, if it is a great technique to help me become an HPO I'll do it, no questions asked".

4. Which companies would you recommend to be looked at due to their particular approach to Performance Management and their subsequent results?
This is a difficult question, because as soon as you call a company high performant it goes down again. However, I would say

Sometimes, people think performance management is all about money and the bonus part. Yes, it is a part of this as well, but the bigger part is aligning everything from top to bottom.

Ziggo. It is a cable company which used to call themselves an LPO (Low Performance Organization). About four or five years ago they were crucified on business televisions because they were so bad and they had received many complaints. They started to work with HPOs, they implemented a performance management system and they are now the best performing cable company of Netherlands and probably of Europe: highest profitability, highest client satisfaction, highest employee satisfaction. Why? Because they painted the picture of how the company could be. They did not even call it HPO, they called it HPZ (High Performance Ziggo), and they started asking all the people in the organization "How are you going to help us create this HPZ?" So I think Ziggo is an excellent example. They are now merging with UPC, as UPC is also interested in becoming an HPO.

5. How can an organization ensure it has an efficient approach to Performance Management?

We now know many things about the structural instruments we can use. The Balanced Scorecard, the Performance Prism, and there are also tools for sustainability now. I firmly believe in the behavioral sciences. People are very difficult. If you could just take a mold and implement it, there would be no problem. If you want to ensure a good approach, spend a lot of time with your people, spend a lot of time on the wbehavioral factors, get to know what is important in their behavior and how you can influence that behavior. It is better to implement a system that is not perfect, but with excellent people, rather than the other way around.

6. What do you think of the emerging trend of using personal performance measurement tools?

I believe it is a nice idea, because if you look

at the term performance management and at the use of performance indicators you get "indicators of your performance", so when using these tools you get some indications on your health, sport performance and so on. But as my grandmother used to say, if it is "too", it is not good. So if you use them too much, there is a problem. Sometimes, people measure everything and do not have time to live anymore. So use them in moderation. And it is nice, because you can make the analogy with the organization, it is the same thing. Use these tools with moderation, don't measure everything, don't spend 100% of the time on this, just look at the indicators, base your decisions on them, look at the results and change your actions if needed.

Rahul Deo Gupta
Corporate Head of Strategy, Planning, Operational Excellence, Abunayyan, KSA

Through The KPI Institute's presence at the 2014 edition of the Strategy Leaders Forum, held in Dubai, the PERFROMANCE Magazine team was privy to valuable insights and had first hand access to the latest thoughts and trends in strategy formulation and execution, organizational performance and business excellence.

Our correspondent, present at the event, caught up with internationally acclaimed business leaders and senior strategy professionals in a set of interviews that brought up inspiration and experienced advice on developing and executing competitive and sustainable business growth strategies.

One of the valuable opinions on strategic planning and performance management came from Rahul Deo Gupta, the Corporate

Head of Strategy, Planning and Operational Excellence at Abunayyan.

1. What does the term Performance Management mean to you?

Performance Management is actually about aligning everything, from the strategy right to the performance of the people, so you are aligning each and every person in the organization to the strategy, and this is what performance management means. Sometimes people think performance management is all about money and the bonus part. Yes, it is a part of this as well, but the bigger part is aligning everything from top to bottom.

2. What is the relation between Strategic Planning and Performance Management?

Once you have the strategy, you have objectives and Key Value Drivers, the areas in which you need to excel, you measure those ones. Measuring means there has to be an owner for those measures. So you connect everything in the PMS with those measures. And, again, as it cascades down you have all the people aligned to that and they are measured against that. This is one part of it. The other part is the "how". How do you achieve your objectives, how do you excel and the initiatives you have for that. Of course, there will be broad initiatives and milestones, so you will have the ownership of the milestone and the ownership of the initiative as well. All these things link and you get a total alignment, and that is how the strategy and performance management actually work.

3. How do you see the disciplines of strategy and performance management in your geographical area today?

First of all, I will talk of the Kingdom of

As we could say, culture eats strategy for breakfast, so culture is very, very important. Again, I would strongly recommend an approach from the very top. The tone set by the top management, not just the owner or president or CEO, but the entire leadership team, can make or break the culture.

Saudi Arabia, where I come from as of now. Here, performance Management is still in the early stages of development. Many organizations have gone a long way in that, so they have tied up everything, the bonuses and the performance of the individuals, but I would say that how you tackle performance management is also important. Measuring if the target is 100 or 500 is not the only thing that you get from it. So the approach towards this needs refining all across the country now. There are circumstances that will help you achieve your targets or not. So how do we take care of that? How do you look at the initiatives management, from the performance point of view? These are aspects that could be improved. So this is now the state of performance management in KSA.

However, 17 years of my career were in India. There, I feel that performance management has evolved and is now at a very, very mature state. So it is like performance management is a given. This is the difference between the two countries I have worked in.

4. Which are the main challenges organizations face in developing strategy and managing performance?

First of all, in strategy, in the context of Saudi Arabia, most organizations have evolved in an opportunistic manner. We can say their strategy was opportunistic. After the second and third generation of family owners have taken over, now there are strategies in place, people say "No" to certain things, like moving from the steel industry to food or something else. My organization did that, because there was an opportunity, now we look at some other options. We realized which our core competencies are and we decided to take a look at that. The challenge here is in making the senior management say

no to these things and to get buy-in from the top. Especially when you have family businesses. The focus used to be "what is good for the family is good for the business", but now it has changed to "what is good for the business is good for the family". Also, before the accent was on family owned – family managed businesses, but people realized they do not have the capabilities, so now we're talking about family owned – best managed businesses. People like us were hired to do this. So I think these are the challenges many organizations face.

In performance management, again, another challenge is that companies, at least in KSA, don't look on their companies on the long term, they think about the short term, unlike India. If you think on the long term, this might help in the employee retention and give people a holistic long term view of the whole performance management of the company.

5. What advice would you give to practitioners working in this field for overcoming these challenges?

The first one is the help from the top management, be it the CEO, president or owner. He should have 100% buy-in, 110% buy-in if possible. So the top management needs to be educated. He needs to set the correct tone to everybody. The way he presents these tools makes or breaks the whole thing. Also, he should have the right team on board, both in terms of capabilities and mind set.

6. Which were the recent achievements in generating value from performance management in your organization?

I can narrate a few. Before we implemented a performance management system, everyone was doing what they wanted. Then, we have strategically defined each

employee's perimeter of action, so the first, very important thing is that we eliminated the competencies overlap. Secondly, the performance of the organization as a whole has increased, because there is a big deal of alignment, which means people know what initiatives to take against what is measured, so they are really focused. The 80-20 rule applies – they are focusing 20% of their resources or efforts to get 80% of the results. So there is a high focus. These are the most important two advantages of using a performance management system.

7. What would you recommend as an approach for building a performance oriented culture?

As we could say, culture eats strategy for breakfast, so culture is very, very important. Again, I would strongly recommend an approach from the very top. The tone set by the top management, not just the owner or president or CEO, but the entire leadership team, can make or break the culture. If I am really convinced, I can say "Yes, this is what we should do", while if I am not convinced I will say "If somebody else told you, please do it", so the difference comes from communication things. Communication plays a vital role in building the culture, right from the top, where it should start. There is no such thing as over-communication. This is one part. The other part is the leadership, when it comes to not walking the talk – I say something, but I do something else. This totally destroys the culture. So leaders should walk the talk. These are some pieces of advice that I could give.

Understanding the Big Data, advanced analytics and what it means has evolved, and we are getting to a point where everyone is talking about it, they are doing it consistently well in a number of industries and it is starting to show impact...

Tor Bøe-Lillegraven,
Head of CCI Business Consulting, Denmark

Present at the 2014 PMA Conference, held in Aarhus, Denmark, the PERFORMANCE Magazine team was able to access valuable insights from some of the most highly skilled and experienced academics and practitioners in the field of Performance Management.
Tor Bøe-Lillegraven from the Copenhagen Business School and head of CCI Business Consulting, gave an interview were he spoke about the essential role of big data, the emerging trends and subsequent challenges within the field of Performance Management.

1. In your opinion, which are the main challenges organizations face today in Performance Management?

This is, obviously, highly dependent on the industry and the company. In the media industry, which I know very well, there are two issues. First of all, organizations get very "set" in their ways over time, which means people know how to do their business, so any change will become a challenge. The second one is the idea of being able to measure change and performance. For newspapers, for example, this is a fairly new and fairly innovative thing. Let me give you an example. Usually, or historically, newspapers will measure their sales and readership on a quarterly basis. This gives them the horizon on a quarter and by the next quarter hopefully they will try to do something if the readership or sales were poor. This has completely been turn around in the digital age, because you can get instant feedback on whatever you published online, instant feedback on the user performance that generates ad revenue and so on. Adapting to this data and using it in real time and in strategic thinking is very challenging, both for leaders in firms

but also, obviously, for the employees. Some people have a taste for this, some want to use information to make better decisions and perform better, others see it as an unwanted side effect basically of the need to perform well financially.

2. Which do you believe are the top trends in Performance Management for the year 2014?

This is, again, relative to the industry and the company. But obviously, what everyone is talking about is Big Data. I think we are moving beyond the password and start seeing more practical applications. I think that more industries and firms are understanding what it entails and, in my experience, we are talking about three different things: firstly, there is the idea of having Big Data available (data about customer transactions, production, output etc.), secondly being able to mine that data and analyze it to get something useful from it, and thirdly how to use that data to actually make the best business decisions. And I think the challenge for most industries and firms is how to position themselves in all these three aspects. For some companies, the answer will be that "No, we will not get into Big Data, we will outsource that. We might also not be interested in getting into advanced Analytics, it is not for us, but we would surely like to have the information on the table, to make business decisions". This is what leaders have to navigate in now. Understanding the Big Data, advanced analytics and what it means has evolved, and we are getting to a point where everyone is talking about it, they are doing it consistently well in a number of industries and it is starting to show impact and I think that for 2014 and beyond, it is going to be something that every firm has to address in some way. We are talking about strategic planning for the next 3-5 years, and this will

be a big thing, for sure, I can't think of any example where this could not be applicable. I just saw yesterday a presentation on "Lean production in the apple industry in New Zealand". Will they be interested in Big Data? For sure.

3. Which companies, industries or functional areas would you recommend to be looked at, due to their particular approach to performance management and subsequent results?

There are two industries I would point to. Firstly, there is the Pharmaceutical industry. A lot of things are going to happen there, and basically the types of data they have access to are very interesting. Test data, sales data, all kinds of interesting data. The second one is the solar energy industry. There is a lot of movement in there right now and there is going to be a lot of money shifting hands from the producers of solar technologies to the consumers, power companies etc., and I believe this will be a very exciting business to look at, from the Big Data and advanced Analytics point of view. These are the two examples I would point to and, obviously, in the industry I work most with, the media industry, there are many things going on. Basically, today, a publisher and the media industry can know every little detail about your digital news consumption patterns. And that can be a good thing, because they can tell the content to you and basically get your attention and make ad revenues from this, but there is also the chance of getting too much data, and I think that is one of the challenges we are seeing particularly in the media industry.

4. What 3 pieces of advice would you give to an organization, about managing its performance?

From my experience, when firms want to implement some type of performance

I think the main idea is to make sure that your performance measurement and management system provides you with at least two things: feedback, like going to a doctor and receiving a health report – and foresight, to introduce you into what you should change

management, let's say in the context of the news industry, they look at KPIs, at what makes sense to them. So, for instance, for a reporter they will look at the number of words, number of stories filed, instead of looking at how many Facebook likes a story gets. And one of the challenges when setting these performance measures is that the management has to be a couple of steps ahead of the organization and very "in tune" with the market. So this is one basic challenge that I would point to.

A second one is that it represents an investment. It takes attention, money, investment. In the Big Data example, you have to invest in some data warehouse type of solutions, Business Intelligence type of solutions, and also invest the time to sit around, look at this data and consider it before finding business solutions. This is a third type of challenge I see in implementing performance management. But then again, at the end of the day, what choice do you have? We have been doing Performance Management for quite a time now. It is evolving, it is changing, but it is also getting better and we have better tools at our disposal to make decisions.

5. What is your opinion about the emerging trend of using performance measurement in your personal life?
I will point back to one of my previous answers: it is not for everyone. I think that, for the people who have acquired the taste for it, these are excellent tools. I think that for other people, they can be counterproductive. Performance management is not for everyone, but for the ones who know what they want to do and know what they are doing, it is a great thing to have more tools to help them measure performance.

When it comes to being counterproductive, from my experience, for some employees, working for 2 weeks on a single piece of

content makes it of a tremendous quality. It will be read everywhere and bring value to the company. If you start measuring those people, basically looking at time spent, hours, minutes, that is going to deter them to not have the time to do the stuff that generate real quality. This needs to be balanced, and one needs to be careful when putting in place KPIs. Another trend that I have seen is that of management by numbers and, in my experience, I would be careful in implementing those types of measures in an organization if I didn't really know the value chain in detail.

Rick Edgeman
Professor of Sustainability & Enterprise Performance, ICOA, Aarhus University, Denmark

Given The KPI Institute's presence at the PMA 2014 Conference, the PERFORMANCE Magazine team was able to interview some of the most highly skilled academics and practitioners in the field of Performance Management.
Rick Edgeman, Professor of Sustainability & Performance at the Interdisciplinary Center for Organizational Architecture (ICOA), Aarhus University of Denmark, spoke with the PERFORMANCE Magazine team about sustainable enterprise excellence

1. In your opinion, which are the main challenges organizations face today in Performance Management?
First of all, performance management is, as its name says, a matter of management, so organizations should have the right thing to manage first. So they need to have a well-established organizational design, or at least they need to try. This is why the theme of these conferences is designing the High Performing Organization, which involves

so many factors: the human ecology of the enterprise, innovation and sustainability aspects, performance measures and so on. But I think the main idea is to make sure that your performance measurement and management system provides you with at least two things: feedback, like going to a doctor and receiving a health report – and foresight, to introduce you into what you should change, or more specifically what you should change into, what is your direction. The organization itself should have its strategy formulated relatively to the competitive context.

2. Which do you believe are the top trends in Performance Management for the year 2014?
I would actually give you a different answer, namely for the year 2024. But for 2014, people are still trying to come out of the economic down turn. So people are still focused on making sure they perform well financially. In the same time, there is an increasing pressure to be responsible. They face this exodus of customers that now say "I really like your product, but I don't like your behavior". So I think the current reality is that they still have to be very careful with financial performance, because most companies are still trying to recover, but the future is a different issue. In the future, of course enterprises will need to perform financially, otherwise they will not remain viable, but their performance has to be very evident, while considering the areas of social responsibility, societal results and impact.

Results and impact are not necessarily the same. It is about being economically and environmentally sound. So we can sum it all up to society, ecology and financial-economic performance. This has become a complicated aspect. The environment is very important, and we are rapidly dematerializing the Earth. We have, of course, material costs, but naturally, as the materials become rarer, their cost will accelerate, so we have to find a way to dematerialize. If I were to buy something from you, I would take all of the wrapping off and hand it to you and say "I don't want the wrapping" – this is the dematerialization, finding ways to charge for your services and not necessarily for your products. It is making sure that the company is responsible for every product that they produce all the way from the beginning through its life cycle and after its use. I think this would be the major trend.

We have all of these global challenges, we have extreme climate change, global warming aspects, extreme weather events, drought, desertification, as well as both an aging and a growing population, so proportionally fewer people to be able to provide for a larger society. With aspects such as increasing heat we also have increasing conflicts, we have a situation where the currency today is not really Pounds, or Dollars or Euros, it has become water, food and energy. And enterprises have to find ways to understand and conduct themselves in terms of these real currencies instead of the ones that are more artificial or represent something different. Of course, we cannot ignore the Dollars or Euros, but we have to take into account much more deeply the other currencies.

3. Which companies, industries or functional areas would you recommend to be looked at, due to their particular approach to performance management and subsequent results?

I think we can look at a company like SAP. It is not only that they have this excellent strategy and performance management system, but also that they impact other companies: they estimate to have influenced over 30% of the world's energy use. They have found ways to help you, as an enterprise, manage your energy consumption and other elements, of course. So they contribute not only to you as an enterprise, but to the world more broadly. So SAP is, in my opinion, a very impressive company.

If you look at companies like Microsoft, some of their strategies relied on taking products that were previously existing and transforming them into services. One of our keynote speakers was Joseph Williams. He has only been the dean of a business school in the United States for the past year. But he was also a managing director of Microsoft, over more than 10,000 employees. His last assignment at Microsoft was that of a managing director for software as a service. So they are truly changing the way things are happening. And this has implications for performance measurement and management. We have to understand much better how we can measure service provision, service performance. We are very good with tangible, physical things, which we can put our hands on. We are much less good with ideas, as they are much more difficult to measure.

4. Which would you believe are future directions for research in Performance Management?

I would say sustainability over and over, because most of my research is in enterprise sustainability. Of course, I have interest in ecological and societal sustainability, but as a member of the Business School, my interest is mostly in enterprise sustainability, and understanding how it connects to all dimensions of enterprise performance. It is not just about optimization, because the strategy that I follow to optimize my performance in one area may render me vulnerable in other areas. So I think I should simultaneously consider at least three things, and one would be the excellence domain, the international quality process. This usually means excellence, in many performance domains: the human capital of the organization, the operations, the supply chain, the innovation performance, the financial performance.

But there is more than excellence in the way organizations perform. They need to protect themselves, they need to make sure they can be resilient, that when facing an extreme challenge they can find a way to bounce back from that challenge and recover their health. They need to find a way to make themselves more robust, so that whenever a shock does come to the system, they can overcome it. The thing is that robustness, resilience and excellence are, probably, consistent for the most part but they are not identical. The set of policies, strategies and partnerships that optimize one of those three will not optimize the other two. So enterprises really need to consider how to determine the best mix for them. And then they need to be able to develop those Key Performance Indicators (KPIs) that will help them accomplish that. Because, if they do not have those KPIs to move forward to, they will be guessing. And maybe it will be a wonderful guess, but maybe it won't. So they really need to have that information, they need to be able to develop those measures. If you ask me how healthy I am, I might say "I weigh this much", or "My resting heart rate is this one". I might say many things, so one question can have many answers. One of them is probably a better answer than the others. We need to find better and then the best answers, better and then the best KPIs, so that we can achieve better and then the best performance. But then the questions are "Where do you want to perform?", "What is important to you?". So, it is also about determining the KPIs that are consistent with your enterprise values.

5. What 3 pieces of advice would you give to an organization about managing its performance?

Consumers are increasingly concerned about organizations being socially and environmentally responsible. So they must manage their operations, they must manage their policies, they must be transparent in ways that allow consumers to determine for themselves, to apply their own KPIs to decide "is this company responsible or isn't it?" and to make decisions on those bases. If they don't make that available, customers will increasingly assume they are hiding something. And they will find a company that hides nothing instead. I believe it is very important to have solid indicators for transparency. It is important not to have a "rubber stamp type" of organizational governance, which would just say "Yes, we approve". Instead, the governing board should be doing its real job, namely to make sure that the company is performing in a responsible way. Companies have to make sure they are relevant. You can do the wrong things incredibly well. And by wrong things I do not necessarily mean bad things, just things that nobody cares about. So you can do really well something that nobody cares about. I can really use chalk on a chalkboard really well.

We need to make sure we do the relevant things, those things that make a real difference, and we need to make sure we are not only measuring results – results are easier to measure than the second thing, which is actually more important – the impact. What is the difference that it makes? It is important to measure performance by results. It is even more important, I believe, to make sure you connect that to the impact, because this is what you want from the indicators – feedback, foresight and for them to reflect whether you, as an enterprise, are doing something important

Consumers are increasingly concerned about organizations being socially and environmentally responsible. So they must manage their operations, they must manage their policies, they must be transparent in ways that allow consumers to determine for themselves, to apply their own KPIs to decide "is this company responsible or isn't it?" and to make decisions on those bases.

and making a difference. Each of us has children, and those children will have their children and so on. So, what should be important is the legacy we leave as persons? We should be focused on how our grandchildren will remember us, on whether we have made a positive difference in this world. At some point, enterprises don't think at that legacy, and they should be thinking about it, because they are leaving something behind every day. They need to make sure they are moving in the right direction. So, it is all about relevance, responsibility and, in general, sustainability, because most organizations want to continue to exist, they want to prosper. Everyone wants to prosper and to be regarded in positive ways.

At the end of your life, you will not say "I wish I had worked more", you will say "I wish I had spent more time with my children", "I wish I had donated more of my time to this cause" – those are the things you are going to think about. And I believe enterprises should start thinking more in the same way. They need to say "Can we make a positive difference, and can we do this in responsible ways?". It is wonderful to provide energy to people in areas that have been energy starved. But not if you do that in a way that creates significant pollution problems. I don't need to go in the deepest, darkest parts of the world and give them a lot of coal. I might solve a part of their problems, I might provide energy, but I will create a new problem by doing that. And this is part of the significance of these global challenges, they are complicated. You solve one thing and you create a new problem, or you ignore one. Because the complexity is so great and the other relationships are so complicated that I think you need to have KPIs that really examine those complex interactions between factors and that help you move in the right direction.

6. What is your opinion about this emerging trend, of using performance measurement in your personal life?

It is very interesting, we need to have those indicators, they really help us monitor our performance, whether it is personal or at the enterprise level. I don't monitor my heart rate, for example, but I do monitor other things. I will give you an example. I have a friend, Sean. About 15 years ago, he was the president of Excellence Ireland, and before that he had been the president of the European Organization for Quality. Every year, he would take his family to a retreat, and the entire purpose of that was to better understand their interactions with one another. Were they doing everything they could to build their family more positively? Was Sean performing well, and what things did he need to change, so he can be a better father and husband in his family? What did his wife need to change? What was she doing that she could do more of or that she should keep doing, because she was doing it wonderfully well? In the same time, what about the children? This is a different level, but it does have the personal implications, along with the very important family dimension. So, what they actually did every year was building a new family contract, and they would have their own performance indicators for how they do as a family.

So I believe this trend is important. I think that those people who do well in their personal lives, formally or informally, are going through self-examination and self-assessment, all at the time. Not as formally as within the International Quality Awards, for example, which were about enterprise self-assessment, of course. The purpose of those systems, whether it's the American or the European program, was to boost competitiveness, not even between individual companies, but on

larger scales, country performance. This is why the Baldrige Awards were founded in the US, to improve national performance on the global market. There were only a few companies that would apply for the award, but you could see hundreds and hundreds of thousands who would look at the award's criteria, the models, the measures and would apply them to their own organizations, in order to improve them. They didn't care about the prize, but they did care, just as every enterprise does, about improvement.

In the same way, I think this is what people want to do. You don't get up in the morning and tell yourself "I really want to do bad today", "I want to be sick today" or "I want to get in a car accident today". Nobody does this. You are probably not so formal in the way you determine how you want to move forward, but I think there is a trend, people start doing that more and more commonly. This is why people go to the gym, or to personal trainers, and ask how their physical performance or health can be improved. So we see trends like this one, and it is only a matter of time until this branches out to other areas of life. And when people start doing that, they might not even see it as self-assessment, but they are using it to manage their lives in different ways. I love what Danish banks do, because they categorize automatically all the purchases that I make when I use my bank card. Because they do this, we can monitor how we are doing: Are we using too much energy this month? Did our food bill go significantly up or down and why? We can use these sorts of indicators to manage our personal lives. So I think there are trends when it comes to monitoring personal and family life, that are coming from the KPIs we use in performance management and measurement systems. We will be witnessing many changes in this field.

THE KPI INSTITUTE MEMBERSHIP BENEFITS

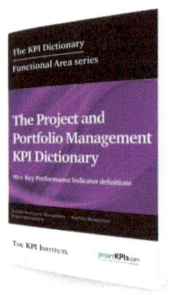 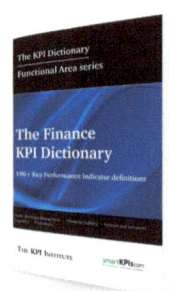 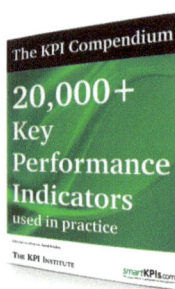    

Research content

▸ smartKPIs.com platform

smartKPIs.com is an online portal containing the largest collection of well documented KPI examples, supported by a community of tens of thousands of members.

▸ Top KPI Reports

Top KPIs series is an extensive annual collection of reports dedicated to analyzing the most popular KPIs across major functional areas and industries, containing thorough analysis of each KPI example.

▸ Performance Management Toolkits

The Toolkit series represents pre-populated templates configured in Microsoft Excel and PowerPoint: Strategy Maps, Scorecards, Dashboards, Portfolios of Initiatives and Employee Performance Plan templates are examples. They are available in editable format and have an instruction manual attached for easy configuration.

▸ KPI Dictionaries

Considered the most comprehensive publications released to date by our research team, they include over 8,000 examples of documented Key Performance Indicators, complete with definitions, sub metrics and calculation formulas.

▸ Webinars

Designed as one-hour long audio and slide-based presentations, The KPI Institute's webinars address key topics related to Strategy, Performance, KPIs, Data Analysis, Data Visualisation, Innovation and many others related to Performance Improvement. Experienced analysts, with a track record of research applied in practice present such webinars on a weekly basis. Recording are subsequently made available on The KPI Institute's eLearning platform.

▸ Research library access

A rich repository containing a variety of research publications ranging from global and regional research studies to fact sheets, catalogues, infographics and generic templates. It is regularly updated with new content as released by our research team.

Event discounts

Get exclusive discounts to our training courses, conferences and forums scheduled throughout the entire year across 6 continents.

Networking

Join your peers! Get and share valuable insights on performance related subjects within The KPI Institute Community.

Professional confirmation

Consolidate your personal brand by using our exclusive badge to demonstrate your professional commitment to performance excellence.

Research helpdesk

A member of our research team will guide you through our knowledge platforms to identify the best information and resources according to your needs.

Research analyst consultation

Benefit from dedicated services provided by our research analysts on 12 practice domains. Find below a list with examples of advisory services covered. Based on your specific needs, customized solutions will be provided.

Advisory services

▸ Strategy
▸ Performance Improvement
▸ Performance Measurement
▸ Employee Performance
▸ Balanced Scorecard
▸ Data Visualization

▸ Data Analysis
▸ Benchmarking
▸ Customer Service Performance
▸ Innovation Performance
▸ Suuplier Performance
▸ Personal Performance

MEMBERSHIP OPTIONS

Practice domain	TKI Membership **$390 per year**	TKI insight+ Membership **$2,900 per year**
*smart*KPIs.com platform*	**Full access to all premium content**	**Full access to all premium content**
Top KPI Reports	**2 reports of your choice**	**All available** currently 127 reports
Performance Management Toolkits	**2 toolkits of your choice**	**All available** currently 9 toolkits
KPI Dictionaries	**2 dictionaries of your choice**	**All available** currently 14 KPI Dictionaries
Webinars	**2 webinars of your choice**	**All available** currently 34 webinars
Research library access	**Preview to executive summaries**	**All available** currently 57 resources
Event discounts		
Preferred rate at training courses and conferences	**$100 off early bird rate**	**$100 off 2 or more participants rate**
Networking		
Network among peers in a private group available only to TKI members	Yes	Yes
Professional confirmation		
Electronic certificate of membership demonstrating the commitment to professional excellence through learning	Yes	Yes
Research helpdesk		
Guidance to explore the TKI knowledge platforms	Yes (online)	Yes (phone)
Analyst consultation		
Video / phone advisory support from TKI research analyst	No	8 hours **
Customized secondary research project on demand	No	8 hours **
Estimated value of benefits if accessed individually:	**$1,500 USD**	**$15,600 USD**

* Access to all 12 practice domains platforms upon their release
** Hours to be accessed when needed by scheduling as per member preference.

Join Today!
www.kpiinstitute.org/membership
The KPI Institute Customer Service
Monday - Friday
+61 3 9028 2223
office@kpiinstitute.org

AUREL BRUDAN

a lifetime dedicated to performance

▌ **DIANA ZĂRNESCU**

"In a world dominated by consumerism, the appeal of science in education and professional practice should be nurtured more."

Born in Romania, Aurel Brudan was never meant to remain tied to a single country, nor to a single continent. His working experiences have taken him throughout nations spread on the entire globe, from Europe, to Asia, North America, Africa, and Australia.

In between his travels, Aurel accumulated over 16 years of Enterprise Performance Management experience, 12 years of Balanced Scorecard expertise on design, implementation and maintenance. More than 20 Balanced Scorecard implementations, with over 100 different performance scorecards and dashboards, stand proof today that Aurel Brudan is a man driven by performance.

It was 11 years ago that he built the foundation of what was to become The KPI Institute, the organizational representation of Performance Management, as Aurel Brudan envisions it. As a CEO today, Aurel tackles issues of Performance Management on all levels of the company, thus showing himself, and all of those in question, that the quest for improvement has only a beginning, but no end.

All this while, Aurel kept a strong tie to his educational journey as a PhD. Candidate and a tutor for the "Managing in Contemporary Organizations" subject within The University of Melbourne, Faculty of Business and Economics.

Some would refer to Aurel Brudan as an educator, others as an advisor, or as a practitioner. But, above all, he is a man driven by ambition and belief in improvement. He encourages others and, most of all, himself, to strive for performance, to think beyond the routine, and to use education as a window towards what we seek to achieve.

The Performance Magazine editorial team searched to get insights from Aurel Brudan, the man who, although could already be described as accomplished, will never stop to draw the line.

Taking the first steps on the Performance Management path

Aurel Brudan began his professional journey as an economist, obtaining a leadership position with the non-profit organization AIESEC. It was here that, for the first time, he became familiarized with the concepts of strategic planning and performance measurement. And thus, upon the completion of his graduate program, he went on to support the implementation of a Balanced Scorecard system, within an Australian public sector agency.

The implementation process continued with the support and supervision Aurel provided, as he decided to prolong his stay and operate the new management system. Showing great interest in the discipline, Aurel chose this path to forge a career, initially by doing doctoral research on the topic of performance management systems, and subsequently by doing research, training, and consulting in the same field.

Ultimately, he started out as a practitioner, carried on to become an educator and this, naturally, led to advisory services. This triangulation of three roles is what leveraged his professional development.

His interest in continual education stems from a deep appreciation towards scientists, people Aurel admires for their commitment to knowledge and education, seen as a means to improve oneself, as a rational being. In his own words, in a world dominated by consumerism, the appeal of science in education and professional practice should be nurtured more.

In this sense, the works of Anthony Stafford Beer, together with the entire literature on systems thinking, had triggered Aurel's interest in this particular field, and he was able to envision the bridge it created towards the discipline of performance management.

Thus had Aurel Brudan began his journey within the Performance Management domain. He regarded his earliest experiences with designated tools and processes as challenging but, at the same time, intellectually stimulating. Years later, when he was assigned a Balanced Scorecard implementation process, he remembered those first lessons which, in spite of their difficulty, ultimately proved useful.

A personal approach to Performance Management: 3 perspectives on one system

Aurel Brudan came to regard Performance Management as a series of actions which, altogether, ensure that the results obtained are also the desired ones, while perpetually improving the extent of these results, and the efficiency with which they are obtained.

Aurel talks about 3 main aspects that would recommend a Performance Management system, above all others: clarity, focus, and improvement.

Clarity, as all the people involved have a clear vision of which results should be achieved, ideally.

Focus, so that what matters, at a specific moment, remains in sight.

Improvement, as all processes, along with their results, are reflected objectively, making further necessary measures become obvious.

However, there are obstacles on the road to performance. As Aurel admits, obtaining the commitment of all stakeholders, whether they are managers or staff, is a challenge in itself. Moreover, as one problem often leads to another, the lack of stakeholder buy-in is also reflected in resource allocation and, ultimately, in expertise levels.

More than once, as Aurel has noticed over time, poor results, obtained within a flawed Performance Management system, are caused by lack of expertise, backed by a lack of invested resources, and by limited commitment levels coming from management and/or staff.

However, as none of these obstacles is without solution, the Performance Management tools and processes can be improved by enhancing the expertise of those operating them, by ensuring standardisation of these processes (through process mapping, template creation and manuals/procedures use) and by automating data collection.

Still in the realm of ways to improve a Performance Management system, Aurel mentions, as best practices in the domain, cascading the system across all organizational levels, including the employees themselves, and automating the data gathering process, establishing the correct KPIs, which should reflect what truly matters. Additionally, a sound architecture, which links all the tools the system entails, together with committed professionals who operate the system and also seek to experiment and improve it, are key aspects to ensuring the functionality of Performance Management.

An example Aurel has observed, as far as the results of Performance Management put in practice go, is related to the improvements made in the airline industry

"Never stop learning. There are so many things to be discovered, in the same field and in related disciplines."

in terms of performance results and overall profitability. In addition, methods of measuring marketing performance, together with the shift towards online, enhance all processes, while also making them easier to track.

And best practices in Performance Management inherently enhance individual performance. An integrated system is what establishes the connection between performance, learning and compensation.

However, his experience has taught Aurel that people also need room for innovation and diversity.

By providing communication possibilities, organizational transparency and educational opportunities, employees will not only become better performers, but they will also offer their buy-in and trust.

As the CEO of The KPI Institute, but also due to his numerous experiences with organizational environments, Aurel reached the conclusion that the best way for management to obtain the employees' buy-in for the Performance Management system is entailed in a 3-way process: ensuring that the staff has the same understanding of what the system means, a clear vision on why it is needed and, thirdly and lastly, to be transparent as an organization internally, as well as externally, in order to ensure support and commitment.

Outside working hours: managing personal performance

A man who has dedicated his career to performance improvement could not overlook the aspects in this discipline which are also viable to be implemented in one's personal life. Outside working hours, experimentation is key in identifying the optimal combination for each person in particular. There are numerous tools and principles available, but the choice that will provide the best results is a matter of personality, choice, and drive, as Aurel concluded.

So what does Aurel find most suitable for his personal performance and how does he manage it? First, Aurel identified a series of aspects which he considers as important to him and, for each aspect in particular, he keeps track of data, with varying degrees of rigour.

As for the hardware and software solutions, Aurel believes these remain at the enabler status for now, and the main difference is represented by the user's discipline, drive and habits.

The same strategy applies to managing one's work-life balance: since each individual has his own specific personality, each

strategy for managing personal performance is relative. The same way in which different things make each of us happy, achieving this balance is a state that we first have to define for ourselves. For Aurel, this translates into having a balanced approach to how he pursues his goals.

A source of inspiration

But, most of all, his piece of advice, as far as both career and personal life are concerned, is to never stop learning.

There are so many things to be discovered, so many opportunities hidden in knowledge, and so many fields that, even unrelated to the performance discipline, are still a fountain of information one could take advantage of. His personal example is extracting knowledge and finding inspiration in what are, perhaps, curious disciplines for someone with a formation in the field of economics: biology, chemistry, philosophy and history, to the name just a few.

Related to the principle of continuous learning is also the development of content which Aurel, as an educator and a practitioner, cannot overlook. In his own words, he believes that so often today we are consumers of content, yet we generate more value and are rewarded at a greater extent by developing it. Valuable content is born out of a mind which assimilated and filtered knowledge obtained from education, on the one hand, and the experiences encountered across his activities, on the other hand.

Thus, case studies, conference presentations, engaging with peers in community forums, or communities of practice, all contribute to validating ideas, learning and sharing of knowledge or, in other words, the development of the discipline.

3 MAIN ASPECTS OF A PERFORMANCE MANAGEMENT SYSTEM:

Clarity

Focus

Improvement

designed by Freepik.com

THE KPI DICTIONARY · REFERENCE COLLECTION OF BOOKS

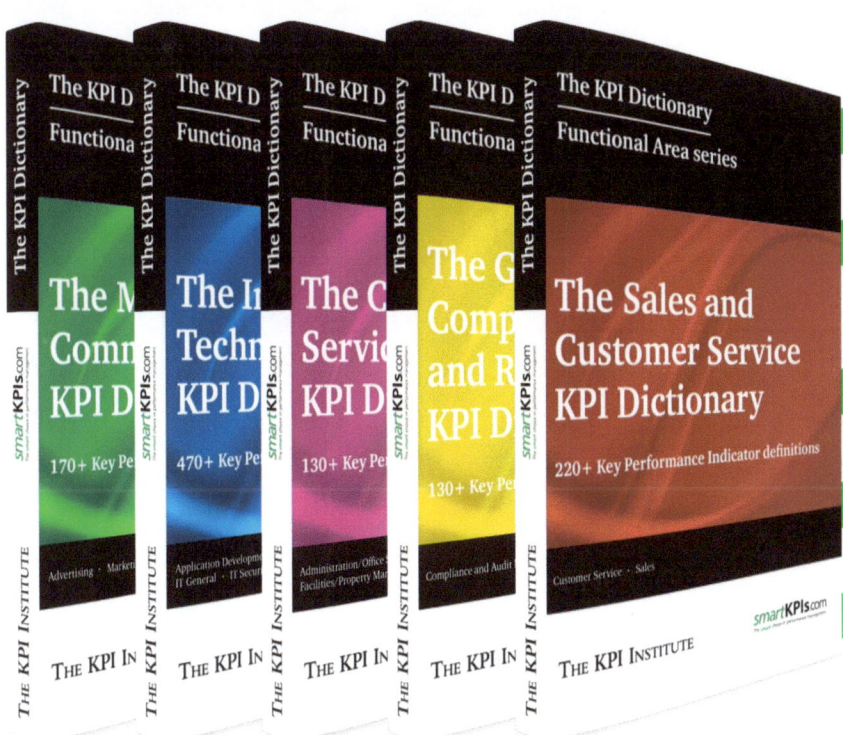

ACCESS
A full collection of KPIs

EXPLORE
KPI definitions, sub metrics and calculation formulas

OPTIMIZE
The KPI selection process

IMPROVE
Your current KPI framework

BUILD
Your internal KPI library

Find the most suitable KPIs to measure your business success!

8,000 + Examples of documented Key Performance Indicator Definitions for an in depth view on Performance Measurement

32 Newly released publications:
▶ 14 Functional Area KPI Dictionaries
▶ 18 Industry KPI Dictionaries

 *7 years of business research invested*

RESEARCH BASED

 *30,000+ resources studied*

PROFESSIONAL EXPERTISE

 *20+ subject matter experts involved*

RIGOROUSLY REFERENCED

More Publications

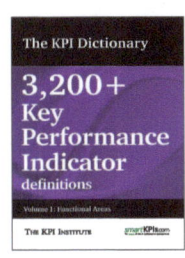
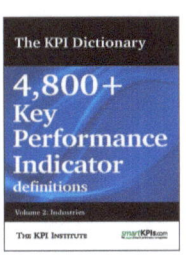

Keep up to date with industry trends and leaders!

PERFORMANCE MANAGEMENT IN THE INDIAN GOVERNMENT: *A brief history*

■ ANDREEA VECERDEA

Performance management as it exists in government includes conventional tools like the budgetary exercise, annual reports published by the Ministries/Departments, performance budgets and the recently introduced outcome budget. Ministries and departments of government have varying practices of periodically reviewing their organizational performance.

Performance Management Division,
Cabinet Secretariat, Government of India

Traditionally, the Indian Government used to be described as a rule-based structure, primarily focused on processes. Such an approach was mainly oriented towards input usage, and performance was assessed against money spent on different projects/schemes. The drawback of this modus operandi was that it failed to look at the results achieved by the activities undertaken by the Government.

In the 1975-1976 period, a scheme of performance budgeting for the financial year was introduced, to analyze the connection between inputs and outputs. More specifically, it looked at:

> Objectives and projects implemented in the past, current and future period;
> Connections between the five year plans and the achievements to date;

> Financial statements highlighting the outlays for the projects implemented;
> Details on the actions taken and achievements in each of the projects conducted.

According to the website of the Performance Management Division (PMD), from within the Government of India's Cabinet Secretariat, in order to improve the functionality of the above presented scheme, a zero-based budgeting approach was introduced in 1980, as well as an outcome budgeting scheme, some years later. Their main scope was to focus more on the results achieved, rather than on inputs.

In 2009, the Prime Minister approved the Performance Monitoring and Evaluation System (PMES) for Government Departments, meant to assess the departments' performance. The system

involves a yearly preparation of a Results Framework Document (RFD), where each department outlines its objectives and the extent to which it managed to achieve them against the targets set. In this way, all important deliverables expected from each department are being monitored, in terms of finance, quantity, quality, short and long term efficiency.

The Performance Management Division, within the Indian Cabinet Secretariat is in charge with the Government Performance Management Systems for Ministries and Departments within the Government of India. According to the above mentioned portal, its main functions include: reviewing and adopting global best practices, updating the existing performance management system and delivering citizen-centric results.

Objective	Weight	Action	Success indicator	Unit	Weight	Target / Criteria Value				
						Excellent 100%	Very Good 90%	Good 80%	Fair 70%	Poor 60%
Promoting administrative reforms in government policies and processes as per recommendations of Administrative Reforms Commission (ARC)	33.00	[1.1] Monitoring and review of administrative reforms recommended by ARC.	[1.1.1] ATR on 125 accepted recommendations of ARC.	Number	4.00	0.2	0.1	00	00	00
		[1.1] Review meeting with the State AR Secretaries on implementation of ARC recommendations.	[1.2.1] Issue of State-wise status report on implementarion of ARC recommenation.	Date	4.00	27 March 2014	28 March 2014	29 March 2014	30 March 2014	31 March 2014
		[1.1] Setting up institutional mechanism in the Central Govt. Ministries and States for regular review of the implementation of ARC recommendation.	[1.3.1] Number of States/ Central Government Minisitries setting up institutional mechanism	Number	4.00	10	07	05	03	02

Value of the Composite Score	Incentive Payment (% of the Basic Salary)		
	Phase 1	Phase 2	Phase 3
	1-3 years	4-6 years	6-9 years
100%	20%	30%	40%
90%	10%	15%	20%
80%	5%	10%	15%
70%	0%	0%	0%

Characteristics of the actual Performance Management system

According to the Performance Monitoring and Evaluation System for Government Departments report, released by the Indian Government's Cabinet Secretariat, the timeframe for reviewing progress towards achieving objectives is clearly defined, and it consists of 3 steps:

> At the beginning of the fiscal year, by the 1st of April, the Results-Framework Document has to be designed;

> After six months, by the 1st of October, progress is monitored against targets, in order to reset goals, adjust priorities and take the actions needed;

> At the end of the year, March 31st, the overall performance is evaluated against agreed targets.

At the moment, 80 out of 84 ministries/departments and their Responsibility Centers are covered by the RFD policy. Below, there is an example of how a year-end Performance Evaluation is conducted by the Department of Administrative Reforms and Public Grievances, as detailed within their Results-Framework Document.

Such a rigorous approach to setting objectives, KPIs and targets supports each Ministry's endeavors to performance. When it comes to setting objectives, it is important to note that they are assigned a certain weight, taking into consideration their priority. Moreover, for each of them, departments have to list the policies, programs, schemes and projects they need to undertake, in order to make objectives real. To measure the performance achieved for each objective, success indicators, or Key Performance Indicators (KPIs) are set, each of them again, with a certain weight attached. Targets are defined on a five-point scale, ranging from poor (60% achievement of the target), to excellent (100% achievement of the target).

Linking the Performance Management system to an incentive scheme

As a consequence of deploying a Governmental level Performance Management system, an incentive scheme is also about to be implemented for the Government's employees. According to the Proposed Guidelines for Performance-Related Incentive Scheme, the incentive's level is calculated based on an established formula, taking into consideration the following aspects:

The maximum amount of incentive payments can be 15% of the Budget savings, and it will be offered only if the department achieves a composite score of 100% (which translates into an Excellent);

No incentive is paid if the composite score is 70% or less.

An example of how an incentive payment looks like for the Head of the Department can be analyzed below:

Incentives' distribution between the Head of the Department, the Head of the Division and any other employees. For example, at divisional level, incentives depend 30% on the Departmental performance and 70% on the Divisional performance. In what concerns the bonus allocated to other employees, each division is free to adopt a different reward scheme, which has to be approved by the Secretary at the beginning of the year. Also, the maximum level of the incentive cannot exceed a certain percentage of the basic salary. It is important to note that each reward is not only linked to the individual performance, but also to the performance achieved at departmental/divisional level. In this way, negative consequences related to targets and rewards are avoided, as individuals are not only monitored against their own performance, but also against the team performance.

It is important to note the great progress the Indian Government has made in the recent years in terms of managing its strategic objectives and taking actions to ensure their achievement. The current Performance Management framework is prone to further changes and improvements, and by the time all 84 Ministries will have implemented the RFD scheme, the overall performance achieved at Governmental level will be better consolidated.

INSIGHTS INTO A STRATEGIC PLANNING PROCESS: *The Abu Dhabi Sustainability Group (ADSG)*

MIHAI TOMA

This strategy marks a shift from the intensity of a start-up phase of building a network and developing the services and processes required to engage our members to being in a position to use the lessons learnt during our first two years of activity to respond effectively to the needs of our members and other organizations in Abu Dhabi to improve sustainability management and reporting.

ADSG, Strategy 2011/2013.
From reporting to action

The Abu Dhabi Sustainability Group (ADSG) was established in 2008 and is a membership-based organization, dedicated to encouraging "co-responsibility in Abu Dhabi to ensure that government entities, business and not for profit organizations are all partners in working towards achieving the goal of economic, environmental and social sustainability," as they explain in the From reporting to action (2011-2013) strategy report.

ADSG's main purpose is to guide its member organizations towards adopting and utilizing best practices in terms of strategy management and reporting. A host to both private and public sector organizations, the most notable members of the ADSG, are:
> The Abu Dhabi National Oil Company (ADNOC);
> The Abu Dhabi Water & Electricity Authority (ADWEA);
> The Department of Economic Development – Abu Dhabi (DED);
> The Health Authority – Abu Dhabi (HAAD);
> The Aramex Abu Dhabi;
> The Dolphin Energy (Dolphin);
> The Etihad Airways;
> The National Bank of Abu Dhabi (NBAD).

Step 1

The mission statement of the Abu Dhabi Sustainability Group is directed at "promoting sustainability management in Abu Dhabi by providing learning and knowledge sharing opportunities for government, private and not for profit organizations in a spirit of cooperation and open dialogue," as mentioned in the above-presented report.

This ambitious mission that has been established is supported by seven main services that the ADSG provides to its member organizations:
1. Improving knowledge (through a portal, a newsletter, publications and seminars);
2. Developing capabilities (through training, one-on-one support, and benchmarking);
3. Sharing experience (through forums and meetings);
4. Facilitating Advocacy (through flagship programs);
5. Building networks (through partnerships with local and international organizations);
6. Expanding the member network (through outreach activities);
7. Reporting performance (through the group's various forums and an annual report).

Step 2

To reinforce the mission of the organization, the ADSG has also established a set of values that are dedicated to transmitting the right message towards all of their stakeholders, primarily towards their employees and members.

It is easily noticeable that the Abu Dhabi Sustainability Group followed best practices in terms of establishing and communicating their values. All three corporate values (responsibility, accountability, and transparency) are accompanied by a definition and a set of 'Principles,' such as coordination, collaboration, complementarity and coherence which provide clarity and purpose to the organization's values.

Due to the fact that ADSG is a membership-based organization and that the bulk of their services and operations are conducted through partnerships with their members and other stakeholders, the next logical step in their strategic planning process was to have a clear picture of the current status regarding their relationship status with stakeholders.

Step 3

To this scope, they have developed a Stakeholder Analysis, a dedicated tool that provides an overview of the different stakeholders, together with their contribution, or impact to areas that ADSG tries to focus on, by establishing strategic objectives.

To facilitate the understanding of this relationship, the stakeholder analysis is grouped into six columns, all of which entail further details on ADSG's expectations and commitments:
> Stakeholder;
> Why we engage? – details here mention

sustainability management and reporting practices;

> Priority issues for ADSG – these include commitment to the company's values, mission, goals and other activities in which they engage in;

> Priority issues for stakeholder – the ADSG follows to improve knowledge, maturity level trainings sustainability performance, and reputation, among others;

> Our Response – this section details what the ADSG offers, in return. Namely, it includes tools and processes such as portals, newsletter, one-on-one support and various meetings.

Following the stakeholder analysis, the next step in formulating the ADSG strategy was to analyze the external and internal environment of the entity.

Step 4

When an organization is going through the process of strategic planning, one key step is scanning its external environment, in order to "take into consideration the business environment in which we operate", as mentioned by ADSG in their report.

To serve this purpose, they have deployed the use of a PESTLE, or the PESTEL analysis. This technique involves scanning the external macro environment of the organization and identifying the Political, Economic, Social, Technological, Legal, and Environmental factors that will influence the achievement of ADSG's strategy.

Each factor, such as the Political and Economic factors, identified by ADSG provides comments that stakeholders can review in order to understand the political and economic developments that may affect the operations of the organization.

For example, the political factor contains the ADSG's comments on Abu Dhabi's Government search for excellence, on the growing local attention to sustainability and on the demand for improved coordination. Meanwhile, the economic factor comprises comments on the economic diversification (which is mostly connected to the Economic Vision 2030 strategic plan), on construction projects (explainable by the boom in economic development experienced by Abu Dhabi), on unemployment and, lastly, on decent work.

Step 5

Further on, by building on the PESTLE analysis, the ADSG proceeds in their strategic planning process towards analyzing the internal environment of the organization. To this scope, a SWOT analysis was conducted.

SWOT stands for Strengths, Weaknesses, Opportunities and Threats, which are, as ADSG mentions, "the key internal and external factors that could help or hinder us from achieving our objectives".

Thus, the organization identified public-private partnerships, sector leaders, multidimensional approach and strategic focus, among others, as strengths, followed by the weaker points constituted from silent members, insufficient resource allocation, representative turnover, levels of commitment and others.

Step 6

The steps undergone up until this point represent the prerequisite steps for formulating a clear strategic framework for the ADSG. The results and insights gathered by following these afore-mentioned steps have provided the basis for creating the main strategic direction of the ADSG, which is represented through its Strategic Goals.

The established goals follow best practice recommendations in terms of standardization as each goal starts with a verb. The goals are also accompanied by the Vision and Mission statements which represent the desired state of the organization, and the manner in which ADSG will reach its desired state.

In terms of recommendations for next steps, breaking down the Strategic Goals of the company in more specific Objectives is seen as a good approach. These objectives would then be clustered and graphically represented in a Strategy Map, a visual representation of an organization's strategy, highlighting the strategic objectives of an organization together with the cause and effect argumentations, linked within the four perspectives of the Balanced Scorecard.

HOW KPIS CHANGED A GOVERNMENT.

A Malaysian approach

❚ OANA GAVRIL

While the barriers to achieving Vision 2020 are considerable, they can be overcome through the dedication of, and collaboration between, the Government and the rakyat. Taking up the challenge, this government has formulated the principles of 1Malaysia, People First, Performance Now as a way to accelerate our performance in order to achieve Vision 2020.

Catalysing Vision 2020 through 1Malaysia,
People first, performance now

Nowadays, due to increasing competition in the business world, most of the firms and organizations are obliged to adjust to new ways of enhancing their performance. This improvement is mainly linked to the implementation of performance management systems, new strategic directions, or important shifts in the strategy of the organization.

Malaysia took into consideration these aspects, especially after being faced with drastic changes within its governing party. Following six decades of performance management initiatives, combined with accountability, planning, and coordination, the results were still not satisfactory for Malaysia. The efforts directed towards increasing efficiency "were extensive, somewhat unconnected, and, until recently, rarely emphasized measurable outcomes," said John Anthony Xavier, professor at Putra Malaysia University, and former director of research in the Public Service Department, for the Tying performance management to service delivery: public sector reform in Malaysia 2008-2011 case study (2011). As a result, the Malaysian government decided to employ Key Performance Indicators (KPIs) as one of their main performance measurement tools.

In 2009, Prime Minister Datuk Seri Najib Razak created a specialized unit to supervise the implementation of the performance management system, naming it the Performance Management and Delivery Unit, or PEMANDU, for short. A detailed overview of the program, designed to present the public with recent results that it has achieved, together with necessary details added to increase transparency.

PEMANDU was established to "oversee the implementation and assess progress of the Government Transformation Program (GTP) and Economic Transformation Program (ETP), facilitate as well as support delivery of both the National Key Result Areas (NKRAs), and National Key Economic Areas (NKEAs)" as stated on the PEMANDU online platform.

The structure of the program was created in accordance with the 7 main areas of interest, named National Key Results Areas, which serve the purpose of creating both short, and long term initiatives in order to improve these sectors. Six ministers have been appointed to lead the mission of fulfilling the six National Key Results Areas (NKRA) which focus on:

> Reducing crime: headed by the Minister of Home Affairs, it includes a number of initiatives destined to descend the trend in crime and to increase public satisfaction of police services;

> Fighting Corruption: assigned to the Minister in charge of Law, within the Prime Minister's Department, aims to prevent resources being taken away from the economy of the country, and it will ensure a fair playing field for all the participants within the economy;

> Assuring Quality Education, which generated a 12-year programme - The National Education Blueprint- ensures short and long term changes in the education system of the country and it comes under the Minister of Education's governance;

> Raising Living Standards of low-income Households, assigned to the Minister of Women, Family and Community Development, it aims to reduce the disparity between the economically advantaged and disadvantaged, as well as raising the income level of the country;

> Improving Rural Development, found under the Minister of Rural and Regional Development's authority, focuses on offering the people who chose to live in rural areas a

healthy and sustainable living;

Improving Urban Transport, which will fix the public transport within the Klang Valley and Kuala Lumpur, as these are the major economical areas is governed by the Minister of Transport;

Addressing Cost of Living, for which the Deputy Minister is responsible, is designed to offer immediate term measures for the living costs of Malaysians affected by the global food and energy prices, while assessing other strategies that will address the rising cost of living within a long term plan.

The purpose of implementing this 7-point program is to ensure accountability among the administration and the civil public service, and to ensure the transparency that each government is looking forward to offer to its citizens. Due to the presence of these National Key Results Area, people can have an objective evaluation of the effectiveness of the leadership and the implementation degree of these strategies.

Together with the National Key Result Areas, the government of Malaysia has defined the vision, mission and objectives of the country for it Vision 2020 strategic development plan, by creating 4 pillars to support its strategy:

1. Malaysia: People first, performance now;
2. Government Transformation Program;
3. Economic Transformation Program;
4. 10th Malaysia Plan. Macroeconomic growth targets & expenditure allocation.

1Malaysia: People First, Performance Now has become the administrative tag line, with highlights on the efforts that the government is putting into achieving the 2020 Vision.

Additionally, the role of PEMANDU is also to support the Unity and Performance Minister in implementing the Key Performance Indicators system, and in helping the government achieve the ideals settled in their vision and become a high income nation by 2020.

Performance management reforms in Malaysia have resulted in improving efficiency within the bureaucratic and public service delivery systems, besides helping the economy function very well in the competitive South East Asia region. The case of Malaysia's government is just another example of how a thoroughly implemented performance management system can help increase performance within any type of organization.

To achieve sustained high growth and high economic wellbeing in the future, Malaysia should create a competitive economy that uses resources efficiently, has sound economic fundamentals, is flexible in responding to global development and is backed by solid human capital, innovation and technological capacity. In this new economy, the private sector must take a leading role through entrepreneurship and must be energised so that it will invest and create new sources of growth. The role of the Government is to provide frameworks conducive to economic development and an efficient delivery system

Dr. Mahani Zainal Abidin, National Economic Advisory Council member. "Developing the Malaysian Model for a Global Economy" in Readings on Development: Malaysia 2057 (2009)

RedBalloon AUSTRALIA:

an employee engagement strategy turning millions annually

■ MARCELA PRESECAN

"Way back in 2001 when RedBalloon was founded, I had so many hopes and dreams for what the business could be. I wanted to change gifting in Australia forever and to encourage 'good times' over more 'stuff.' After working for so many serious corporations, above all else I was intentional about creating a workplace where people genuinely wanted to wake up and come to work in the morning. And well, we must have got more right then wrong because RedBalloon has been a BRW Best Place to Work five times in a row and I am proud to share that under the guidance of CEO Nick Baker we've been officially named one of the world's most democratic workplaces. Making the WorldBlu List of Most Freedom-Centered Workplaces has once again proven our deep commitment to RedBalloon's most important 'competitive weapon' – our people!

Naomi Simson, RedBalloon Founding Director, (2015)

A company that gifts is what one might describe RedBalloon as. It gifts to its customers the opportunity to learn and enjoy new experiences but the focus in this article falls on what it gifts to its employees.

This year, Smart Company awards its 7th place in "The top 20 on-line retailers 2015" to the biggest online gift experience provider in Australia. It is with genuine awe that performance management practitioners around the world should look into the success story behind the numerous recognition titles the RedBalloon Company currently holds. Such companies, like the hereby presented RedBalloon organization, testify for the core driver of performance: the individual.

It is inspiring that, by building on NEF's (New Economics Foundation) "Five Ways of Wellbeing" (2010) - Connect, Be Active, Take Notice, Keep Learning and Give, – RedBaloon has reached a point when its employee-centric organizational strategy is a catalyst for staff engagement practices worldwide.

"RedBalloon was not always a great place to work […]. It was challenging and confronting as we went on our growth

journey. There was much we learned along the way… and ultimately we got more right than wrong and ended up listed as a BRW's Best Places to Work five times.", Naomi Simson, RedBaloon Founding Director, (2015).

So how does Redballoon become one of the greatest places to work for in Australia? How come that, simply by making its people happier, RedBaloon stands out as one of the lead performers in the world? Well, for starters, RedBallon acknowledges its commitment to measuring employee engagement.

CEO Kristie Buchannan proudly presents an Employee Net promoter Score (NPS) of over 80% for the company, in 2014. Secondly, they provide employees with an empowered environment and motivational tools for boosted participation. Thirdly, they take an innovative approach to employee performance by balancing individual KPIs with "personal promises" that emotionally tie the employee to the strategic plan of the company. RedBalloon also spices up its rewards and recognition programs with spontaneity, encourages communication through "team huddles," uses Yammer for internal social networking, and turns

beginners into brand energizers through a unique on-boarding process.

Although it may seem that RedBaloon wins the performance race through sheer democracy, it is the understanding of basic performance management terminology that has allowed the organization to validate its engagement governance:

> Organizational culture is best valued when it is a by-product of employee engagement: "At RedBalloon people come to work as themselves and not as their job titles; as people, not staff. […] We empower our people to make decisions in their roles, knowing there is trust from the business in those decisions, and knowing they are allowed to make mistakes – as long as the learn from them. We exercise freedom in the flexibility we provide for all our people – they are provided with the tools needed to fulfill their roles, which means we have happy people, leading to happy customers, and ultimately resulting in happy profits […]", Nick Baker, RedBaloon CEO, (2015).

> Organizational performance and employee engagement lead to unprecedented achievements when linked to organizational culture, KPIs, and strategic direction: RedBallon empowers all its employees

Engagement Capability is the ability and readiness of an organisation and its managers to successfully engage their staff

RedBalloon, Employee Engagement
Capabilities Report 2013

with the same access to the company's vision, strategy and business performance plan. Company management believes that transparency better enables both team and individuals to actively contribute to the success of the organization.

> Organizational alignment is paramount in the achievement of ambitious company goals: In 2004, the founder of RedBalloon, Naomi Simson, and her team set the valiant goal to provide the company's gifting experience to 10% of all Australians, within a 10-year range. That meant that, by 2015, 2 million people would benefit from RedBaloon's services. However, what seemed impossible to the team, at that time, actually materialized two years short of the 2015 target, as a result of strategic consistency and staff commitment to the company's core values.

> Key Performance Indicators drive strategy and vision throughout the whole organization: In her blog post entitled Six things to do to make sure you have a great day at work, Naomi Simson states that: "At its core well-being is becoming an economic indicator for productivity [...]," thus casting further emphasis on employee happiness as a key strategic driver for performance.

Cascading KPIs gives employees accountability for growth in the capacity of their teams: RedBalloon commits itself to the measurement of organizational – # Employee Net Promoter Score – team and individual KPIs.

> Balancing KPIs prompts employees in also taking ownership for the quality of their results: RedBaloon balances individual KPIs with "personal promises." These are a measure of the individual's contribution to the strategic plan of the organization.

> Reward and recognition platforms are major contributors to engagement outcomes: In their search of a performance indicator that would engage the whole sales team in achieving their targets, RedBalloon came up with the "Wishlist" initiative. It entailed that each of the company's employees create a personal Wishlist with their most desired experiences out of RedBallons' 2500 proposals. Throughout their activity, each employee receives points respective to the achievement of their KPI targets. Whishlists are updated every time employees receive points from their managers, telling them how much closer they are to achieving their dream. In addition, Oscars are awarded to team members that faithfully follow the

company's values, and a Dream Catcher Wall enables RedBalloon managers to commit to a personalized framework for incentives.

There is a point to this case study when we come to ponder on the relevance of # Employee engagement when it comes to performance management. And, if the RedBalloon success story hasn't been enough, here is a quick side-analysis. Engaged employees work in favor of % Staff retention. % Staff retention increases % Employee advocacy which, in turn, leads to elevated chances of attracting key talent into the organization. # Employee engagement boosts productivity, which further impacts $ Sales and $ Turnover in positive ways. Happy employees secure happy customers. Happy customers trigger an increase in # Customer satisfaction. # Customer satisfaction positively influences # Customer loyalty and # Customer advocacy. Because of the growth in $ Sales, $ Turnover and # Customer satisfaction, the profitability of the company skyrocketed. In conclusion, there is one word that summarized the contribution that successful employee engagement strategies make to the field of performance management, and that is…inestimable.

EXTERNAL ANALYSIS. WHAT TOOLS AND TECHNIQUES CAN WE USE?

Porter's Five Forces business management model

PAUL ALBU

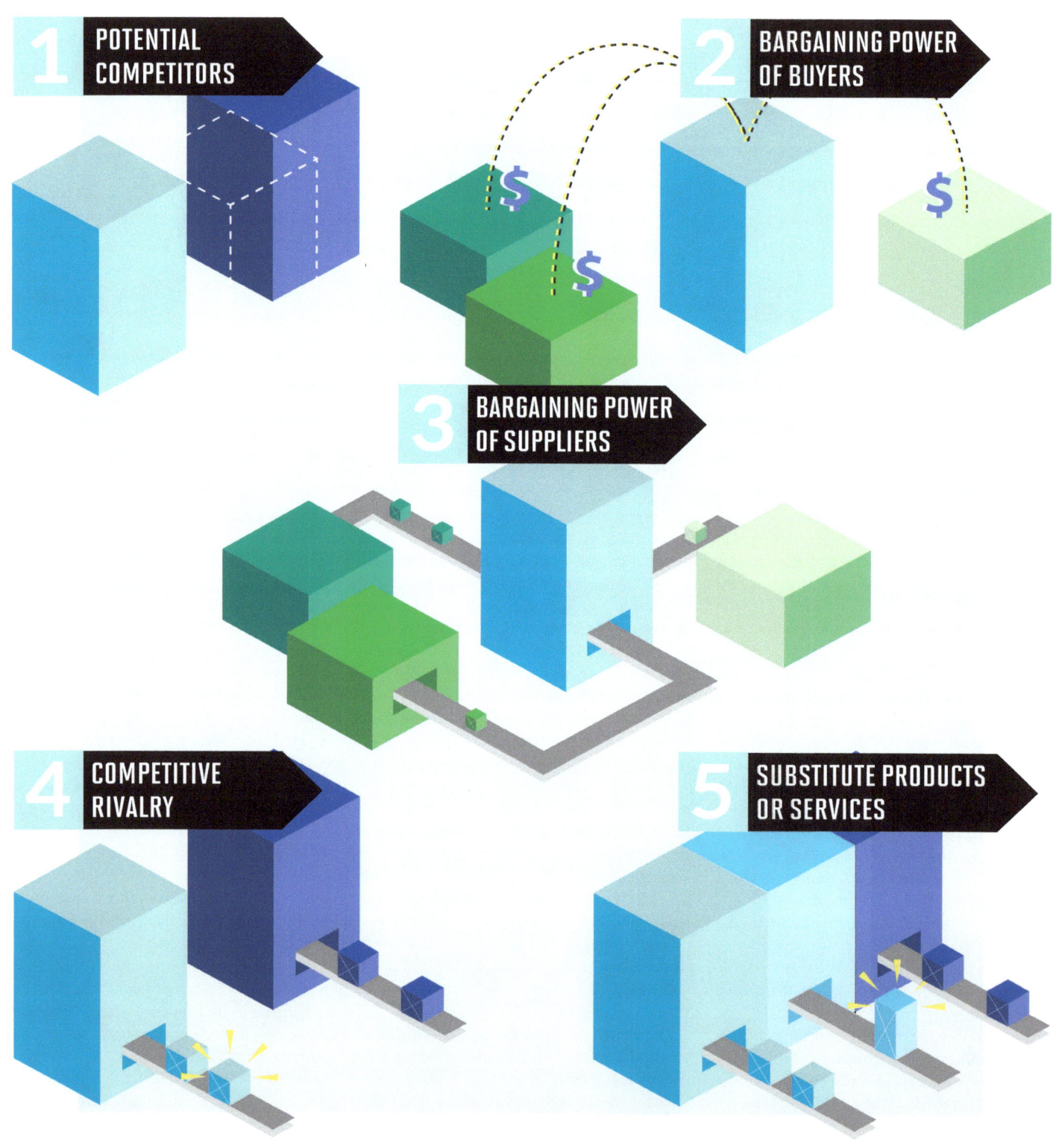

In today's competitive market, having a good strategy can differentiate success from failure. Of course, to a certain extent every company has a strategy regarding the objectives it wants to achieve, but the difference between a successful and an unsuccessful strategy lies in the steps taken when formulating it. As expected, the first step is essential, namely the external analysis. In order to facilitate this process, organizations can deploy a number of tools to perform an external analysis thoroughly.

Many companies nowadays deploy a business model, which may differ from one organization to another. Porter's business model is used by strategy consultants in order to study the threats and advantages a company has within its respective industry.

What is a business model?

To better understand what a business model is, the 2 terms, "business" and "model", can be explained separately, using the accessible definitions provided by the Cambridge Learner's Dictionary:

> Business: the activity of buying and selling goods and services, or a particular company that does this, or work you do to earn money.
> Model: a representation of something, either as a physical object which is usually smaller than the real object, or as a simple description of the object which might be used in calculations.

So, in general, as Alexander Osterwalder (2004) states in The Business Model Ontology, a business model represents an abstract comprehension of the way a company makes money: what it offers, to whom does it offer and how can it accomplish its purpose.

In his article Business Models for Electronic Market, Paul Timmers (1998) defines the business model as:

> An architecture for the product, service and information, including a description of the various business actors and their roles;
> A description of the potential benefits for the various business actors;
> A description of the revenue sources.

Porter's five forces model

Porter's five forces model is a business model that managers can use to analyze the opportunities and threats posed by an industry to a specific business.

As the name states, the model focuses on 5 different forces that can influence the direction of a business. John F. Rice is one of the many theoreticians who explained the five forces, in his 2010 report Adaptation of Porter's five forces model to risk management.

According to the specific literature, firstly there is the risk of entry by potential competitors. They represent companies which are not currently competing in an industry, but have the resources to do so if they choose. A recent example can be Apple, which manufactured computers but entered the phone industry a few years ago it because it had the necessary resources. Companies that activate in a certain industry may prevent potential competitors from entering, because the more the companies, the harder it becomes for an established organization to have the same profits and market share.

Secondly, there is the bargaining power of buyers. In any commercial act, there are 2 type of buyers: the individual buyer (the end user) who consumes the product, or other organization who distributes the company's product to the individual buyer. For example, a company that produces bread can sell the product to different retailers, which will therefore sell the bread to the end user.

If the buyer has a strong bargaining power, it will influence the company to lower its product's price, while maintaing its high quality. This will lead to an increase in cost and decrease in profits for the company. If the situation is reversed, a company can gain an increase in profits by lowering costs and reducing the product quality.

Thirdly, the bargaining power of suppliers can have an extensive influence. Suppliers are organizations that provide inputs to the company. They can supply the company with materials, services or labor. If the supplier possesses a high bargaining power, they will influence the cost of the company's product. Alternatively, the company itself can benefit from the bargaining power, if it is able to choose from a wide range of suppliers.

Rivalry among established companies within an industry is the fourth force in Porter's five forces model, and it refers to the competitors from within the same industry, which can influence the product sold by the company. This can be done by a competitor firm through its product innovation, advertising campaigns, or competitive strategy. To understand, let's imagine that Samsung decided to produce a bigger smartphone, a decision that could also influence Apple to develop a bigger smartphone in order to remain competitive in the market.

The last force refers to the substitutes to an industry's products, the existence of another product within the industry which can replace the company's product. For example, for the companies that were producing alarm clocks, their product was replaced by smartphones, because they have integrated the alarm feature.

In Porter's five forces business model, these forces may have different values for influencing the business. For example, if a rival company lowers its prices, the bargaining power of suppliers force will have less value because the company must adopt a different strategy in order to remain competitive in the industry, be it an aggressive strategy (lowering its product's price), a defensive or a conservative one.

Porter's five forces model can only be a point in deciding what strategy a company should adopt. Other frameworks that can be used to create the strategy of a business are, in John Rice's opinion, the value chain, SWOT analysis, PESTEL or the gap map, tools that shall be explained in details in the future issues.

From satisfied customers to brand advocates

MARIA DESMONS-MACREA

Decreasing the number of complaints by improving the quality of the products, or the services offered – is what a lot of organizations understand about how to do customer service, in particular, and business, in general. But are satisfied customers sufficient for the company's long-term profitable growth? Or do they need something else?

This article discusses the important relationship between customer satisfaction and customer loyalty, and argues that the former should be viewed only as a short-term goal, whereas customer loyalty and advocacy should be the strategic objective of all those organizations that want to differentiate themselves and to ensure their long-term survival on the market. Although the two go hand in hand, the latter should be the ultimate goal of all businesses.

Within the existing literature, there are three main understandings of the relationship between customer satisfaction and customer loyalty. The first one, brought forward by researchers like Anderson, Heskett or Rust and Zahorik states that "satisfaction [is] an antecedent of customer loyalty, which in turn influences the firms' profitability," as noted by Guillame Bodet in his work, Customer satisfaction and loyalty in service: Two concepts, four constructs, several relationships (2008).

The second line of thought, whose main promoter was Pierre Chandon, is mainly focused on the individual re-purchasing intention but, as Bodet also concludes, this is restricted to an individual who only has one purchasing option, so its applicability is limited.

The third group, "tended to reveal a weak or insignificant relationship between satisfaction and repurchase behavior," as explained by the same Bodet.

As stated in above, customer satisfaction should only be an intermediary objective of every organization, whereas triggering a loyal behavior among their customers should be part of their long term / strategic objective.

This assumption is based on the differences that exist between certain attitudes and behaviors of a satisfied customer, versus those of a loyal one. The satisfaction level is, most of the times, related to a certain product, transaction or interaction. As a result, growing the customer's satisfaction can be an easy to achieve target, but keeping it at high levels is a rather difficult task. The satisfied customers tend to stay with the supplier only until a better alternative makes itself present.

The customers' loyalty, on the other hand, describes a behavior, not just an attitude. It is significantly more difficult to grow, but it is very slow to decline as well. This behavior translated into several levels of commitment towards the company, each one encompassing its own benefits.

First of all, loyal customers are prone to stay by their favorite organization's side when the business might not be flourishing. Even more important than that, they will be the ones who will make sure to let others know when things are on the right track in their relationship with the respective organization. The final level of commitment, however, is when they recommend the organization in a proactive manner and out of their own initiative.

This is what we refer to as customer advocacy and it constitutes the basis for sustained profitability and growth, as it allows organizations to predict the behavior and attitudes of their current customers. By being able to do so, they will have an undeniable advantage against those competitors who base their decisions on the changing behavior of a non-loyal pull of customers.

Examples of companies that are recognized world-wide for their loyal customers are: E-bay, Four Seasons, Apple, Amazon, Zappos or Harley Davidson. Fred Reichheld, the author of the The Ultimate Question 2.0 (2011) book argues that Harley Davidson is one of the brands with the highest number of loyal customers, although there are very few research studies that highlight this. This conclusion is based on the fact that Harley Davidson's logo is the most tattooed logo on people's body.

Reichheld argues that co-branding their personal reputation is the ultimate way in which one person can show his/her loyalty towards that brand. This obviously says a lot about the buying preferences, attitudes and behaviors of those customers.

To conclude, both maximizing customer satisfaction as well as increasing customer loyalty should be a target for all businesses which are aiming at a long-term profitable growth. The brand loyalty is directly linked to the repeated satisfaction of customers, and can only be achieved by having a performant Customer Service capability that does more than solely minimizing customer complaints; it gives their customers the right reasons for them to become advocates of that organization!

KPIs
Quality
Efficiency

Software
+
Architecture
+
Interface

Monitoring Healthcare Information Systems with Key Performance Indicators

▌ RAMONA GLIGOREA

Throughout the years, the healthcare industry has become increasingly more complex due to technological and medical evolution and, as a result, it is characterized today by an overwhelming amount of information. Therefore, hospitals require an efficient information system that will enable the proper management of all these requirements.

Investing in hospital information systems

The number of investments in hospital information systems (HIS) has increased, as paper medical records have become cumbersome and difficult to manage. A hospital information system can be defined, according to Karen Wager, Frances Lee and John Glaser Wager (2009), "as a computerized system that is designed to meet all the information needs within a hospital"

The primary goal of HIS is to support hospital activities at different levels, by using computers and other equipment for collecting, processing, storing and communicating both patient related information and administrative data on all hospital activities. Other goals refer to improving staff efficiency, or removing unnecessary procedures.

KPIs for hospital information systems

Monitoring HIS with Key Performance Indicators (KPIs) will help reflect the quality and efficiency of information logistics. There is a variety of KPIs that can be used to assess the technical quality of HIS, software quality, architecture and interface quality and so forth.

HIS
"As a computerized system that is designed to meet all the information needs within a hospital"
KAREN WAGER,
FRANCES LEE AND
JOHN GLASER
WAGER

Information
Management

Some KPI examples are listed below, adapted from a 2009 benchmarking study (Hübner-Bloder & Ammenwerth), called **Key Performance Indicators to Benchmark Hospital Information Systems,** conducted for the Institute for **Health Information Systems.**

Technical quality KPIs
% Health information system (HIS) availability
# Response time of HIS
# HIS data loss rate
# Restore time of HIS

Software quality KPIs
% Functional coverage of HIS software
# Time needed for standard functions
# Software maturity level
# Software updates/upgrades duration

Architecture and Interface quality KPIs
Interfaces between HIS systems
Clinical department using an own subsystem for documentation
Time to connect subsystems that have standard interfaces
Double interfaces

When it comes to selecting and monitoring KPIs to track the performance of the information system they have in place, healthcare organizations should focus on selecting the most relevant ones, specific to their needs and according to the objectives established.

SPORTS PERFORMANCE TRAINING TRANSFORMED:

The German national team at the 2014 World Cup

AUREL BRUDAN

In sports, as in most human endeavors, preparation is the key to success. It is just this time last year that we witnessed one of the best examples in this matter, offered by the German national team (DFB).

It seems that, in preparing for the 2014 World Cup, DFB left nothing to chance. "Naturally it is our goal to reach the pinnacle there. We will prepare ourselves like a world champion. I also think that we, because of the last four years, are among the favourites. We face up to this task and we put this pressure onto ourselves." These were the words of Joachim Löw at the end of 2013, as conveyed in a 2014 article by The Telegraph. They resonate with Tom Coughlin's press conference statement, made before the New York Giants won against New England Patriots in Super bowl XLVI: "humble enough to prepare, confident enough to perform".

What was so special about Germany's preparation for the 2014 World Cup? In one word transformational, not through the ingredients in themselves, but through how they were combined into integrated performance:

1. Environment for team cohesion – custom holiday resort

Campo Bahia is a custom made training camp, complete with housing units, floodlit FIFA regulation training pitch, outdoor swimming pool, spa, and lounge, dining area, fitness center, media center and an auditorium for team meetings. Having all facilities available on site meant avoiding hour long commutes from a hotel to and from a training facility. It also offered privacy and a sense of community among the players. While having their own space, being housed in groups of 6 in a villa, they also interacted in the many common spaces available across the resort. According to left-back Benedikt Höwedes, as quoted by The Telegraph: "This village has been a major factor in building up the special team spirit in the group today.". Reportedly, 23 tons of luggage and equipment were shipped in preparation for Germany's stay during the World Cup tournament.

2. Acclimatization – selecting the right climate to train

With group games scheduled in hotter cities in the north of the country and other games scheduled in the cooler conditions of the country's costal south, the team had to select a base location that would facilitate acclimatization and recovery. It was considered that it would be preferable to move from warmer to colder conditions rather than the other way around, hence the location of the base, 682 miles from Rio de Janeiro.

3. Fitness training – miCoach elite team system from Adidas and EXOS

An advanced physiological monitoring system, miCoach includes a small PLAYER_CELL device worn by the players which measures the speed, distance, acceleration, heart rate, and power of every athlete in training. Data can be immediately analyzed by fitness trainers and the team doctor, as well as post-sessions for in-depth analysis.

Darcy Norman from EXOS presents the potential of learning from such data: "Just as there are many ways to accumulate distance, each position and how the player plays their position during drills, is different. For example, a defensive midfielder may make the effort or accelerate to cover a big distance at speed but may only go 5-10 meters and then have to stop and change direction. In contrast, an outside defender – based on how they play and the team's tactics — may cover a greater distance at speed. Both movements are important and relative to the position. Keeping this in mind, those stats need to be looked at in the context of the game and how the coach wants each player to perform. For a defensive midfielder, we may look at distance in relation to the number of accelerations they made, while we may look at the distance covered, distance at high intensity, and the number of sprints for an outside defender."

Monitoring goes as far as tracking mineral deficiencies, VO2 max (a measure of the body's ability to transport oxygen during exercise), napping patterns and hours of sleep for the previous night, at player level.

Before the tournament, Germany had a 10-day preparation camp in a secluded village about 1,000 meters (3,300 feet) above sea level in the Italian Alps. Training at altitude stimulates the production of oxygen-carrying red blood cells that increase stamina.

4. Determination – Nervenstarke

Shad Forsythe, an American fitness coach working for the German National team through EXOS, declared the following in an interview published in Sports Illustrated: "Confidence comes from knowing that physically they are ready for this.".

The combination of physical fitness and mental strength, was also acknowledged by Alejandro Sabella, the Argentina coach, before the 14 July 2014 final: "The Germans have always shown physical might, tactical powers, and mental force." (The Telegraph, 2014)

5. Game data and analytics – SAP Match Insights solution running on the SAP HANA platform

According to an SAP and DFB joint press release from June 2014, the solution is intended to facilitate the analysis of training, preparation and tournaments. It also intends to enable coaches and scouts to process vast amounts of data to find and assess key situations in each match to improve player and team performance.

Oliver Bierhoff, manager of the German national football team illustrated its potential in number crunching "In just 10 minutes, 10 players with three balls can produce over 7 million data points. SAP HANA can process these in real time. With SAP, our team can analyze this huge amount of data to customize training and prepare for the next match."

Software alone is not sufficient in processing such vast amounts of data. The federation has 40 sports science students helping it sift through data on each opponent, according to Folha de Sao Paulo newspaper.

A system this detailed has never been utilized in soccer before and its debut at the World Cup has clearly been influential. After the completion of the World Cup in Brazil, SAP plans to offer the Match Insights program to other football federations as well as club teams.

On and off the pitch, the German national team's performance at the 2014 World Cup was inspirational. It illustrates key ingredients to success: preparation, innovation, determination. The way they were integrated in the ramp-up of the 14 July 2014 game sets to change the way sports performance training is approached... And not only! P

BALANCED SCORECARD SYSTEMS
One road towards automation

▮ MARCELA PRESECAN

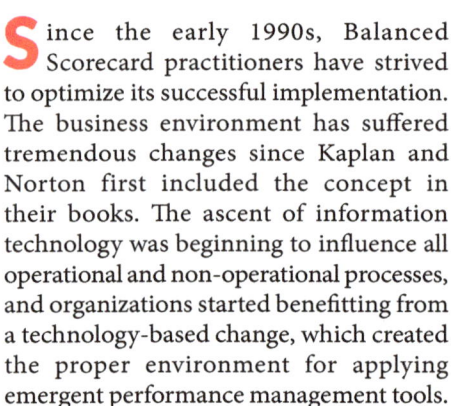

Since the early 1990s, Balanced Scorecard practitioners have strived to optimize its successful implementation. The business environment has suffered tremendous changes since Kaplan and Norton first included the concept in their books. The ascent of information technology was beginning to influence all operational and non-operational processes, and organizations started benefitting from a technology-based change, which created the proper environment for applying emergent performance management tools.

Balanced Scorecard pioneers prided themselves on using spreadsheet-based paper reports to master the functionalities of the concept, without putting pressure on the company's budget. However, the full potential of the Balanced Scorecard was yet to be discovered. The demand for alignment brought the incremental need for cascading the BSC at all levels of the organization. Employees needed to be united in their efforts to achieve the overall vision and mission, as well as the organization's strategic goals and objectives. The organizational Scorecard was, therefore, complemented by the implementation of departmental and individual Scorecards, all of which purposefully communicated data and monitoring results.

The vast amount of information flow became overwhelming for manual processing, while significantly increasing the cost of Balanced Scorecard development, in the same time. Profiting from the rapid ascent of information technology, organizations began to acknowledge the substance of automation.

The different stages and various approaches of Balanced Scorecard Systems' automation have revealed a number of prevalent products that serve this purpose, as adapted from The Microsoft Balanced Scorecard Framework (2002):

> Automated spreadsheets: widely used tools to track performance within a Balanced Scorecard System;

> Balanced Scorecard templates: internally developed Balanced Scorecard designs, created with the use of desktop publishing tools;

> Business Intelligence (BI) Products: Scorecard automation software products that provide the organization with the technological architecture for structured reporting and intricate analysis;

> ERP (Enterprise Resource Planning) Applications: Balanced Scorecard software, which creates extensive databases to facilitate reporting and decision making;

> Balanced Scorecard stand-alone applications: software solution that provides unique presentation layers of collected data and subsequent statistics;

> Balanced Scorecard Frameworks: a complete set of tools and methods designed and developed by software providers to enable the deployment of the Balanced Scorecard Systems at all levels of an organization.

A further analysis into the reasons for choosing one against the other, during the process of implementing a Balanced Scorecard System ourselves leads us to the scrutiny presented in the table herewith.

Automated scorecard solutions are exemplary ways of managing vast amounts of information related to the performance management system of an organization. Although their contribution to an effective strategy execution is significant, they might not always be cost-effective. The small and medium sized business Balanced Scorecard practitioners may be forced to use desktop publishing tools in order to control their spending. Even in the case of larger companies, deploying a Balanced Scorecard System across the entire organization can be costly, when the new releases, trainings and maintenance fees are finally added.

But before renouncing the idea of implementing a Balanced Scorecard proficient software into your organization, consider the fact that such an investment can be beneficial. Building your own Scorecard solution is not without strain. Extensive programming might be needed for efficient data management and collection. Manual data feeding may become inconsistent with business requirements and growing databases, as well as a burden for employees who are unable to supply data for their measures.

Ultimately, Balanced Scorecard automation depends on the readiness of the organization to implement it and to manage information the best way it can, and finds, suited for achieving success. ▪

designed by Freepik.com

	Pros	Cons
Automated spreadsheets	Quick to configure Easily accesible Simultaneous use by multiple users	Multiple versions of the truth Lack of control over data ownership Abiguous user access rights Inability to connect to data sources Limited data sharing
Balanced Scorecard templates	Cost effective Suited to the internal technological structure Creative formatting	A short term solution Feeble structure
Balanced Intelligence (BI) Products	Excellent for collecting and structuring hard data Great with analytics	Directs focus to available data rather than strategic objectives Hard to manage non-numeric information High cost when deployed within the entire organization
ERP Applications	Very good at leveraging with transactional systems Single data source Easy configuration Extensive database	ERP-centric Not well suited for integrating external data Heavy database structure High costs
BSC Applications	Good presentation layer	Limited when working with multiple data sources Do not easily integrate with existing structures
BSC Frameworks	Personalized portals for employees Operational tools Leverage Existing systems Innovative funcitionalities Links to e-mails, calendars	Incremental costs with deployment May require training on proficient use

AUTHENTIZOTIC ORGANIZATIONS:
The solution for low engagement levels

▌ RAMONA GLIGOREA

The importance of individuals' psychological well-being for the proper inner functioning of any organization should be one of the main topics addressed by every manager of this era. And this is directly related to creating workplaces that are healthy, where people find meaning in what they do and are captivated by their daily activities.

Once a year since numerous publications, such as the Fortune Magazine, come up with lists of top most admired American companies, based on criteria such as: the quality of management, innovation, commitment to ensuring a healthy environment and so forth. But does admiration answer the question: Are these companies the healthiest places to work for?

It remains uncertain whether the most admired organizations are also the healthiest places to work in. More revealing, from this perspective, are the best companies to work for ranking, that are also published on a yearly basis and, this time, the criteria taken into account is the employees' great pride to work for certain companies, a sense of camaraderie, trust in management, a sense of meaning, belonging, and enjoyment.

Organizations where you can find all the human needs mentioned above are what the author Manfred Kets de Vries describes as authentizotic companies, in his "Creating authentizotic organizations: Well-functioning individuals in vibrant organizations," (2001) study. According to his theory, the lack of employees' engagement is a recent phenomenon which is closely connected to changes within the working environment.

The label authentizotic is derived from two Greek words: authenteekos and zoteekos. The former emphasizes the idea that the organization is authentic – as a workplace label, authenticity implies that the organization evokes admiration for employees through its vision, mission, values, culture, and its original structure.

The term zoteekos refers to something that is vital to life – in the organizational context, it describes the way in which people are invigorated by their work. Employees in organizations that can be easily labeled as zoteekos feel a sense of balance and completeness.

So what exactly do authentizotic companies do different?

Some of the world's most respected companies – world-class authentizotic companies – are globally recognizable: General Motor, Microsoft, British Petroleum, Wal-Mart, and IBM are just a few examples.

Many of the managers leading these organizations have fostered a strong sense of purpose for their employees, while simultaneously implementing the process necessary for global extension of their business.

On the course of their own search for meaning, these leaders have created a strong vision that clarifies what the organization stands for, highlights the company's fundamental purpose for existence, and recognizes the importance of each employee's contribution to the company's success.

When it comes to hiring new employees, these organizations are very selective, wanting to be sure that the new hires will embrace the values of the company. In an authentizotic company, the management communicates in a clear way not only how things have to happen, but also why they should happen.

Aiming to foster a sense of belonging, these organizations favor an amoeba-type structure, according to Kets de Vries (2001), – when units become too large, they are split, or smaller companies are created, within the umbrella of a larger company structure, in order to form flexible units and allow all employees to relate and interact with each other. Authentizotic companies try to minimize hierarchical differences and become flat organizations, spreading responsibility throughout the entire company.

Manfred Kiets de Vries is his book "The leadership mystique: Leading Behavior in the human enterprise" (2006), presented authentizotic companies as being responsible to provide the "A.I.R." necessary to foster innovation:

A – Give employees Autonomy to encourage creativity;

I – Encourage Interaction between employees to create synergy;

R – Recognize employees' contribution to company's success.

Basic motivational needs, those that we can simplistically label as love, fun, and meaning, are at the heart of authentizotic organizations, as well as at the heart of employees' engagement. A MAGIC formula, proposed by Tracy Maylett and Paul Warner in the MAGIC: Five Keys to Unlock the Power of Employee Engagement (2014) publication, works by encouraging the implementation of measures designed to increase meaning, autonomy, growth, impact, and connection, measures which will eventually lead to employees' high level of engagement.

Because authentizotic companies strive for a low level of organizational stress (the consequences of stress are reflected in high levels of absenteeism, performance decline, conflicts and so on), and help their employees maintain an effective balance between personal and organizational life, authentizotic companies are and remain the organizations we need to hope, and aim for.

THE 5 W'S OF DATA ANALYSIS

▌ MIHAI PĂCULEA

On the road to developing a strategic plan destined to determine and improve either the general performance of an organization, or performance within a particular department, specific tools have proved themselves to be very useful for assessing the current situation, and taking the next logical steps towards achieving the objectives set. One of the most used and most useful tools, when properly applied, is data analysis, due to the clear and precise insights an organization can gain from it.

However, as it happens too often, data analysis is mistakenly taken as a collection of data generated only by a specific cause and reflecting just a restricted segment of a given reality. If this is the manner in which an organization envisions data analysis, then it restricts this tool, without benefitting from the many advantages it can provide.

Still, performance improvement is a continuous process and the manner in which data analysis is used by an organization is not excluded from it. In order to exploit the complete advantages of this tool, a better understanding of data analysis is required.

In the following you can find answers to 5 of the most common questions regarding data analysis, more precisely what it is, why is it so useful, what kind of results it generates, who is the most appropriate person to apply such a tool and, finally, if there is a time when data analysis should or should not be used.

What is Data Analysis?

Briefly explained, data analysis is defined as the process of researching, organizing, and manipulating data in order to bring out useful information.

BusinessDictionary.com expands this concept, defining data analysis as "the process of evaluating data using analytical and logical reasoning to examine each component of the data provided. This form of analysis is just one of the many steps that must be completed when conducting a research experiment. Data from various sources is gathered, reviewed, and then analyzed to form some sort of finding or conclusion. There is a wide variety of specific data analysis methods, some of which include data mining, text analytics, Business Intelligence and data visualizations."

Why we should analyze data?

Data analysis helps organizations extract meaning from available data, transforming a pile of unwieldy information, such as a pile of figures, into valuable knowledge. Data analysis differentiates the scientist from the general population as it prevents him from making largely unsubstantiated claims, or assumptions, often concluded from chance occurrences.

Also, data analysis is not always about statistical significance. A distinction is often made between statistical significance, on the one hand, and practical / clinical significance, on the other hand. Consequently, it is not a matter of statistical significance or nothing at all. After all, anything can achieve statistical significance if the sample size is large enough.

Benefits of analyzing data:

> It shows any significant changes than might have occurred in the dependent variable (KPI) that the organization hoped to influence;
> It uncovers factors that may be associated with changes in the dependent variable (KPI);
> It shows connections between, or among, various factors that may have an effect on the KPI;
> It can offer credible reasons to show stakeholders that the project / program in question is successful or that the organization was able to exceed limitations;
> It can determine reasons/factors that made related work more effective / less effective than expected;
> It helps the organization learn from the past and prevent a recurring set of causes that are known to generate a negative effect;
> It measures the impact of the initiative/ program implementation on the KPI, variable.

What results does data analysis generate?

Data analysis outcomes can be divided into 3 main categories:

a) Short-Term Outcomes: the most significant part includes change in the skills, attitudes, and knowledge of the decision makers / influencers.

b) Medium-Term Outcomes: this sub-category consists of changes in behavior and decision making.

c) Long-Term Outcomes: long-term outcomes mainly comprise the persistence of behaviors and broader lifestyle changes.

Who is in charge of data analysis?

The most appropriate person to conduct the data analysis process in an organization is the Data Analyst who is responsible with the analysis of performance measures, process optimizations, cause analysis, as well as with drawing reports for decision makers.

If the organization does not have a Data Analyst, the next most appropriate person in a company is the departmental manager, who can analyze data and create reports, either for decision makers or for themselves, as a department.

When you should use data analysis?

Data analysis can be used whenever an organization, or a person needs to take the best decisions based on facts, to better understand the causes that have led to a negative / positive impact on the performance measures, to gain in-depth understanding of a process flow, to discover how to optimize a process, how to minimize the risks or mitigate them etc.

When appropriately analyzed, data always offers clear and precise information which highlights the path that must be taken in order to reach the desired results. Data analysis comprises succinctly valuable knowledge, supported by facts. Otherwise, when this tool is ignored or misused, such information may be found spread over an unnecessary length. The danger, in this case, is that it leaves room for interpretation and might lead to possible erroneous decisions. P

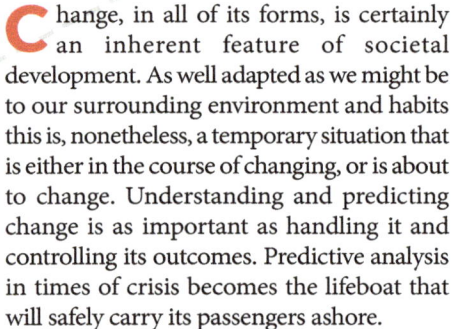

designed by Freepik.com

PREDICT FUTURE CRISIS BY RECOGNIZING ITS CHANGE-PATTERN

DIANA ZĂRNESCU

Change, in all of its forms, is certainly an inherent feature of societal development. As well adapted as we might be to our surrounding environment and habits this is, nonetheless, a temporary situation that is either in the course of changing, or is about to change. Understanding and predicting change is as important as handling it and controlling its outcomes. Predictive analysis in times of crisis becomes the lifeboat that will safely carry its passengers ashore.

Understanding current changes

Pinpointing the meaning and course taken by contemporary changes is a shot in the dark situation, blurred not only by incomplete access to information, but also by the interfering subjectivity of those involved. Thus, it becomes obvious why some of the current controversies repeatedly fail to be dealt with, such as the battle for global warming recognition. Such cases also highlight the impossibility of grasping the real consequences these changes will bring along. If the results of global warming, for example, could be envisioned before they will come into existence, perhaps more counter-reactive measures would be imposed to reduce the aftermath effects.

The question that arises, at this point, is where, and how does a company fit into this context? An organization today is infinitely more exposed and more sensitive to changes than the individual is. Therefore, it should be prepared to face not only internal crisis, which crisis management mainly focuses on,

but should also be aware of all the potential external crisis lurking around the corner.

The importance of the change pattern

When changes occur, which they do, they disrupt the status quo equilibrium, and measures need to follow suit in order to readjust the situation, and reach a renewed state of balance. Predicting and preparing for changes will not prevent them from happening, will not even guarantee success, but they will, however, reduce the time of reaction and eliminate the surprise element which produces confusion during the decision-making process.

The change sequence pattern tells us that things happen in a cycle of linked events. Furthermore, each type, or sub-type of change enables a prediction of additional patterns of societal response to change, namely, uniformities of societal behavior in relation to change. By knowing the pertaining culture of an organization, the surrounding environment and its extremes, any leadership team can gain a greater control of changes that are yet to happen.

Types of change and stages of development

There are four types of changes known to man, as provided by Lowell Juilliard Carr in Disaster and the Sequence-Pattern Concept of Social Change (1932), namely: population changes, cultural changes, relational changes and, finally, catastrophic changes.

No matter what type we are dealing with,

comparative and analytical studies, such as the above-mentioned paper, have brought to surface a sequential pattern that each change brings along. It consists of 4 individual phases that reoccur with every change.

The initial phase of change is called a precipitating or initiating event, and it is considered to be a trigger which enfolds the ensuing episodes. The trigger event disrupts the balance. This is the second phase, entitled dislocated adjustment. Traditionally, this stage is the one that, ultimately, makes the difference between successfully controlling such a situation and completely failing to grasp it. It is a phase of chaos and confusion, nonetheless, when true, good leadership becomes obvious and indispensable. The following phases refer to readjustment and renewed equilibrium, and are heavily dependent on how the second stage has been dealt with.

The dislocated adjustment phase

Catastrophes, whether man induced or natural, are the single events that clearly highlight the sequences recognized in change patterns, mostly due to the reduced timeframe between event occurrence, action and reaction.

The tragedy surrounding the World Trade Center event has cast, at some extent, a shadow on the prompt reaction of the New York emergency response departments. However, their crisis management strategies have reduced, even if to a small extent, the proportions of an even greater disaster. The

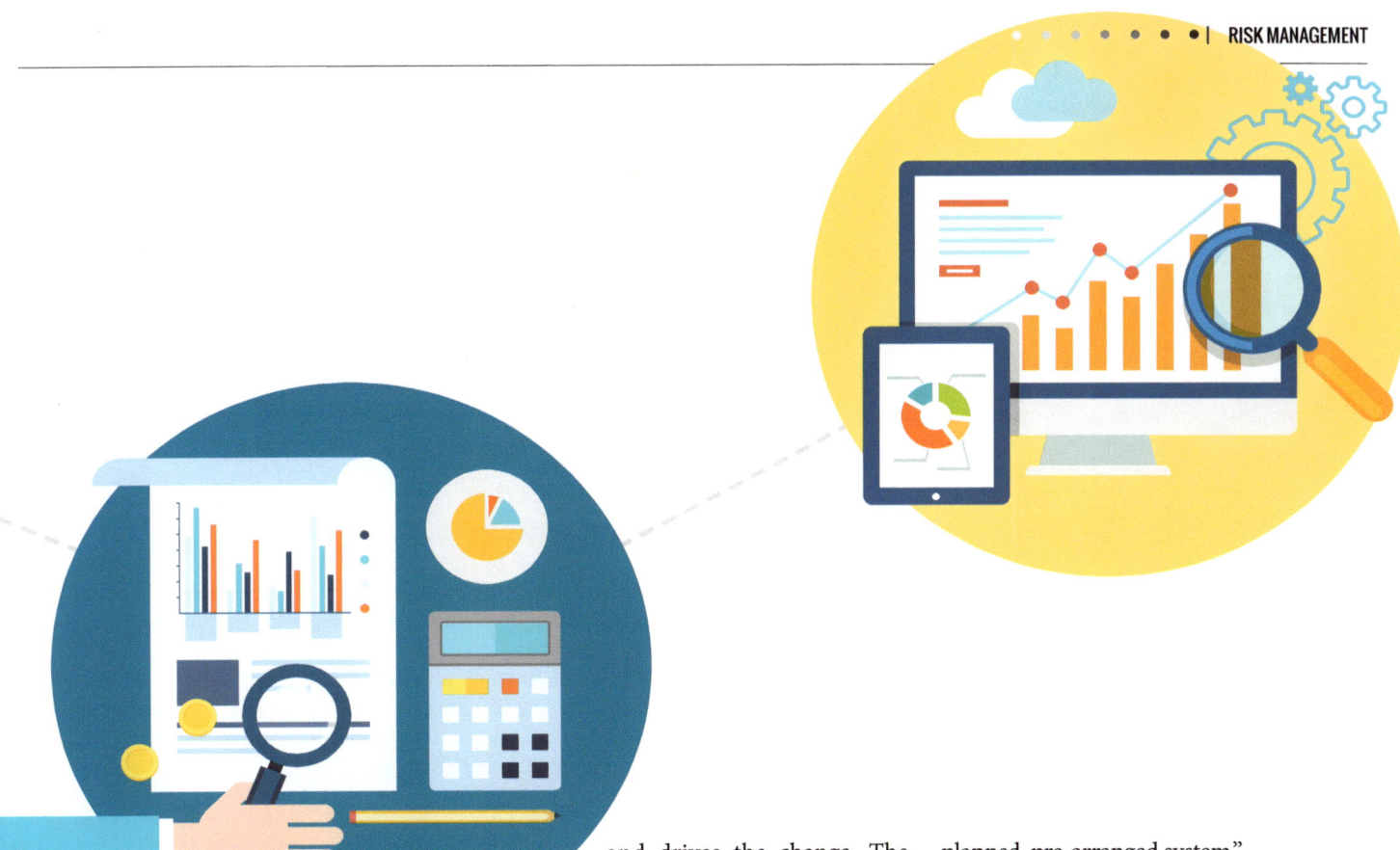

2015 Sewol ferry capsizing, however, is an example of the impairing consequences that slow response to change brings along. Because authorities were unprepared and reacted slowly, a possible search and rescue operation was compromised, giving way to grim consequences.

The above examples, although unconnected, reveal the result of reactive measures taken during the second phase, the dislocated adjustment sequence. In the first case, the time since the triggering event occurred, until the time when corrective measures were taken, was extremely little. Hence, the situation was handled as best as it could have been in this given case, and the level of preparation for such events was satisfactory. In the Sewol ferry case, however, the time of reaction was large, the level of confusion was high, and the measures taken failed to reduce the extent of the catastrophe.

The conclusion that arises from these events is, as Carr points out, that "the manner of reaction after any type of change relies on a society's culture, morale, leadership in addition to the speed, scope, complexity and violence of change."

Change control challenges

Some might question as to why the focus in the change pattern isn't concentrated on the triggering event, the first phase that generates and drives the change. The argument here is that the driver of contemporary changes is very hard to pinpoint.

Even though, in some cases, such as natural calamities, the driver is obvious, most of the times, however, it remains hidden. The precipitating event can be represented by everything from a declaration of war, to something less obvious, like a birth, a death, or a public speech. For this reason, statistical analysis of historical data is of no predictive value, as it cannot rely on lessons learnt from past events and experiences.

Although no organization, or any other entity, can prevent all changes from taking place and disrupting their equilibrium, some measures can still be set in place to increase the level of preparation, to reduce the time of response, and to provide the right decisions, at the proper time. However, it is impossible to sketch a standardized strategy of response to suit all types of changes, as aspects may vary according to culture, geography, and nature of the occurring change.

A change management framework

The EU provides an extensive framework of its attempt to control, as much as possible, events that have not happened yet, in its "Improving aftermath crisis management in the European Union" (2012) report. The purpose is to "reinforce effectiveness, efficiency, coherence and visibility of EU disaster response, shifting from ad hoc response to a (more) predictable, pre-planned, pre-arranged system."

The report provides a framework and further recommendations for an extended range of possible changes that might strike EU's nations in the future, alongside preventive measures, reactive measures and so on. However, EU's Crisis Management Commission points out that its plan is, and must remain, flexible, in order to continuously incorporate new strategies, new techniques and technologies as they are developed and tested.

However, the report is dense as the possibilities of potential crisis hitting EU member nations are numerous, to say the least. The important aspect here does not fall on the measures selected or the classifications made, as these are disputable according to their circumstances. The most important aspect is that it is vital to keep this framework open to include new technologies, new measures, but also new risks that arise in time.

Ultimately, change is unavoidable and it will eventually strike. What happens next, however, can be controlled, either successfully or not. Preparation is the central idea in such cases, as it will close the gaps between the time when the change is triggered and the time when measures are taken. Additionally, preparation, alongside the existence of a coherent strategy, reduces the pressure of the moment and eliminates the confusion surrounding unexpected events. Thus, decisions implemented further-on will, more likely, provide the desired results. P

THE 4 RULES
FOR DESIGNING EFFECTIVE DASHBOARDS

MANUEL HILA

Designing an individual graph may prove difficult, to a certain extent. The degree of difficulty increases considerably when faced with the challenge of designing a dashboard. This is because a dashboard combines a large, often dissimilar collection of information, which can easily become cluttered.

Defining dashboards

Dashboards are, by definition, a visual interface that provides at-a-glance insight into key measures that are relevant to a particular objective or business process. Essentially, a dashboard has three key attributes:

> It displays data graphically;
> It only displays data that is relevant to the dashboard's purpose;
> It contains predefined conclusions, relevant to the dashboard's purpose, and relieves the reader from having to perform his own analysis.

Designing dashboards

Before starting to design a dashboard, regardless of what its objective might be, a prime key step will be to collect user requirements. These user requirements include defining your audience, data sources and key performance indicators (KPIs), along with refreshing schedules, data governance and so on.

As dashboards can be effective and can provide the user with the required information, the question becomes: *How can you design a dashboard that works for you?*

There are several best practices that need to be taken into consideration when designing a dashboard.

Choosing the KPIs that matter

Keep it visual

Allow users to explore

Update Regularly

A first consideration when designing a dashboard is to identify and choose the metrics that really matter out of the vast sea of metrics. For selecting the few metrics that have the privilege of occupying a spot on the dashboard, the following questions need to be answered:

> How does the metric contribute to the purpose of the dashboard?
> Can the data, either internal or external, shed light on the monitored processes?
> Can the metric be designed to measure those contributions?
> Can the metric be built as a systematic and on-going means of measurement?

To enhance the viewer's information absorption, the dashboard could be enhanced through increasing the speed with which data is comprehended by others. This prompts for displaying the information in a visual manner, rather than number-based tables or text. It also provides an aid in decision-making.

Some of the most common visuals used in dashboards are bar graphs, line graphs, heat maps, and scatterplots that have a bigger impact on the viewer, mainly because they are clear, intuitive and people know how to read them. Also when designing dashboards, emphasize on the use of colors, shapes, lines, thickness, and other precognitive attributes that our brain instantly recognizes. For this, you need to research what colors, shapes and sizes will compliment your content and illustrate it appropriately.

A step further in designing an effective dashboard, provided that it already has relevant metrics and is visually engaging, is to offer the opportunity for the viewer to dive deep in the presented data.

As everybody is looking at the metrics' visual representation, each person may have unique questions about what they see. Therefore, create the dashboard in a manner that allows users to interact with it and get the answers they seek.

There are numerous possibilities for this, like the option to filter views, adjust parameters or to provide a historical overview.

Ensure that the metrics which deserve a spot on the dashboard are constantly and correctly updated to reflect current business results.

An effective dashboard allows viewers to make faster and smarter decisions. These decisions are based on the data presented in the dashboards which, if outdated, is no longer representative or relevant for the current situation. P

TIB At A Glance

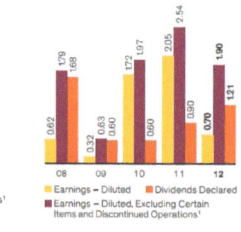

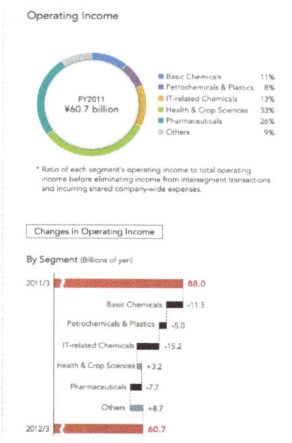

M-HEALTH AND DIGITAL GAMES:
innovation for a new era in healthcare practice

▌ ANDRADA-IULIA GHEȚE

Considering all the fast emerging trends in the information and communication technology areas, we have found that our society is in a fast-paced race to implement e-health systems, which guarantee improved healthcare services for patients and communities worldwide.

What is E-health?

The World Health Organization (WHO) defines e-health as the transfer of health care and health resources through electronic means, but its terminology varies, from health informatics to healthcare practice using the Internet.

It is generally composed out of three main areas, as enlisted by WHO:

> The distribution of health information for both professionals and consumers, via Internet and telecommunication means;

> The benefits extracted from IT and e-commerce aimed at public health services progress;

> The adoption of e-commerce and e-business methods in health systems management.

The forms in which E-health can be transmitted are various, and they can be comprised out of health applications for smartphones, cited as m-health or mHealth. Mainly, these focus on the use of mobile communication devices for health and information purposes, but also on mobile health applications.

Digital games designed to help children with Type 1 Diabetes

Mobile health (mHealth) is a sub-category of eHealth and it encompasses medical and public health practices supported by mobile devices. The field is emerging at a very fast pace and there are about 100,000 mHealth apps at the moment, all available on various platforms.

Digital games represent an important advancement of mHealth currently available to consumers. It became achievable through the combination of Internet and mobile devices. The use and effect of these intermediates between medical specialists and games have been researched by Maged N. Kamel Boulos et.al., in their "Digital Games for Type 1 and Type 2 Diabetes: underpinning theory with three illustrative examples" (2015) study.

Type 1 diabetes is a chronic condition that generally evolves in childhood and requires insulin administration on a daily basis. Therefore, children with diabetes need rigorous monitoring of their diet and blood sugar levels, as well as a rigorous self-management. Sometimes it is very difficult for the family to be aware of all the data and be informed at any time and anywhere.

For this purpose, special mobile and desktop game apps and platforms have been developed, one successful example being the product launched by Ayogo Health. Monster Manor is a free game that helps families with children with Type 1 diabetes to be aware of their children's testing and logging schedule. The game is designed as a health management toy that combines the monitoring need with having fun.

Monster Manor is a game with an integrated diabetes tracking app and, whenever children access their diabetes information regarding blood glucose levels, they receive a reward in the form of a piñata

to crack open in the game. This will help children collect more monsters, or buy new pets for their monster. This is a nice way to reward children for their efforts, encourage them to properly manage diabetes, and also offer parents the chance to monitor them, on a daily basis.

Even if it can be relatively easy for children to cheat and introduce erroneous values only to receive game rewards, the game seeks to inspire supervised children and engage them at a higher level with respect to diabetes testing and information monitoring. The scope of the project was not to obtain correct monitoring information from children, but to engage children in working individually on this matter, while also being monitored (as the software is also installed on parents' devices, who can check on all the data provided by their child).

Using this type of digital games, children and teenagers with diabetes can now handle their health problems much easier, through the gamification of disease management. It's no news anymore that gamification and all kind of social in-game components can motivate patients and help them change their habits and lifestyle.

During the last few years, an emerging need for improved cyber-security and regulation has been emerging and, as such, there is a high demand for particular resources for secure mHealth and eHealth solutions. The advancement brought to life quality improvement for patients is widely recognized, as they can now benefit from an active health self-management system, which allows them to become more independent through these self-assessment, or remote monitoring solutions. P

SETTING PERSONAL GOALS.
Decide what you want to achieve and go for it!

ADELINA CHELNICIUC

No organization can now function without having clearly established goals, and this is generally accepted. However, although the importance and benefits of setting goals at the organizational, departmental or even individual level are broadly known, understood and agreed upon, when it comes to setting personal goals, people have mixed feelings. Is this useful or just time consuming? How can you set both bold and realistic goals? How can these goals be achieved easily?

First of all, why establish personal goals?

In their paper Goal Setting: A Motivational Technique That Works!, Professors Edwin Locke and Gary Latham (1984) emphasized the benefits of setting goals in the organizational context. According to them, performance is boosted when setting goals, as they exert different functions, from the directive to the energizing one. So, why not apply the same principles when it comes to setting personal goals? By adapting the Goal Setting Theory to the personal context, the following functions can be established for personal goals as well:

1. Directive: personal goals help individuals direct their attention and effort toward those specific activities that are relevant in their attempt to achieve those goals. Consequently, all effort that would otherwise be invested in other activities is now consciously directed towards specific purposes.

2. Energizing: bold, daring goals require more effort than the lower ones. Therefore, when establishing a specific goal and understanding its priority compared to others, people tend to dose their efforts for achieving it.

3. Motivational: having clear directions should offer people the motivation they need to achieve the established directions. However, there is a strong interdependency between goal setting and motivation. On the one hand, setting goals boosts your motivation into achieving certain results but, on the other hand, goals should only be established after understanding the inner motivations, as goals cannot reflect something that the individual has no wish or impulse in achieving.

What should you consider when establishing personal goals?

1. It is now generally acknowledged that, within organizations, the objectives should rely on the company's strategy. In personal terms, the strategy can be translated into your self-envisioning elements, such as the life purpose, as well as the personal mission and vision, and they should be established while keeping your values in mind. The purpose of clarifying these, for yourself, is making sure that your goals lead to achieving the desired state in a given time, while moving away from all most unnecessary distractions.

2. In order to have a better focus on the aspects that you want to improve, goals

> *The simple action of setting goals is pointless if it is not part of an entire process of improving your personal performance, be it related to career, social life, family, personal development, well-being or all of above.*

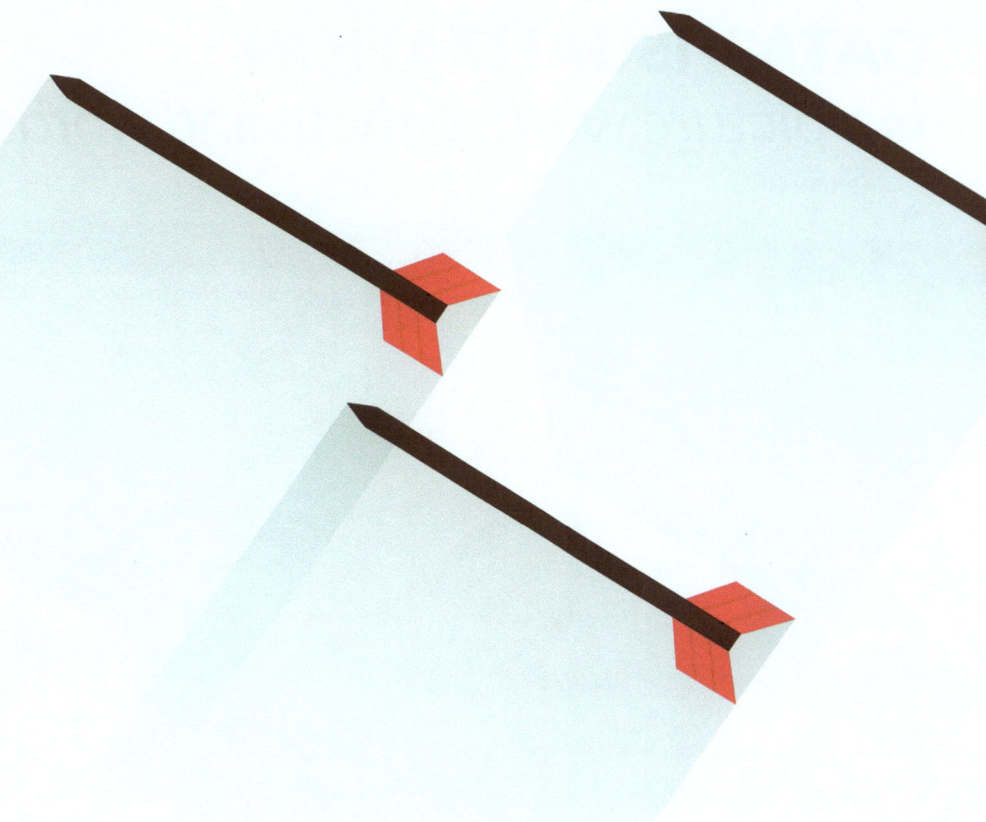

designed by Freepik.com

should be set for all key areas of your life, from the physical, social, emotional and spiritual dimensions to the financial and professional ones.

3. Make sure your objectives are measurable! If you set abstract goals, you are unlikely to be able to keep track of their level of attainment and, therefore, you risk losing focus and stepping away from the respective goals' achievement.

A simple and useful approach is decomposing a SMART (Specific, Measurable, Attainable, Relevant and Time-bound) objective, in such way as to make it easier to be tracked and, therefore, attained. Let's take, for example, the SMART goal Improve my English skills in one year, by undertaking 4 English classes per month. It can be illustrated, in a simpler manner, as follows:

Objective – Improve English skills
+ KPI – # Classes per month
+ Target – 4
+ Timeframe – 1 year

As seen, Key Performance Indicators (KPIs) can be established for your desired goals, as their results will enable you to take the actions needed. Using KPIs gives you clarity, focus on what matters and will support your personal improvement process.

You have set your personal goals. What comes next?

The simple action of setting goals is pointless if it is not part of an entire process of improving your personal performance, be it related to career, social life, family, health or all of the above.

Three simple rules can be applied for increasing the effectiveness of your personal goals:

1. Keep track of your objectives! Sometimes, it becomes difficult to extract the essential from the multitude of thoughts that cross our minds every day. Make sure you remember your objectives exactly, ideally by writing them down and returning to them whenever you need to regain focus on your path to success.

2. Establish an action plan and stick with it! Once you have set your goals for a specific time frame and you have established the way to measure their attainment, you have to take actions in order to reach the desired state. For example, if your career goal for the next five years is becoming a Performance Manager within an international company, the first actions you have to take are either optimizing your CV and online professional profiles, researching for companies that fit your needs and values and applying for the desired job, given that you already have the needed skills, or taking measures directed towards developing this capability, in case you don't.

3. Review your objectives whenever necessary. Even if we talk about attaining those goals and moving on to a superior level or just readjusting goals that don't fit your mission and vision anymore, objectives should be reviewed in order to get the maximum of benefits out of this practice.

Setting personal goals, far from being a time consuming, pointless activity, is one of the first steps that you should take into consideration when deciding to improve your personal performance. Applicable in all areas of your life, goal setting can make the difference between performing at your real capacity and wasting precious time and energy. Therefore, take the personal goal setting process for what it is: an impulse you offer yourself, for your own well-being! P

DATA VISUALIZATION
Is a picture worth a thousand words?

▮ MANUEL HILA

In the words of data visualization expert Edward Tufte, "Graphical excellence is that which gives to the viewer the greatest number of ideas in the shortest time, with the least ink, in the smallest space."

On both personal and professional levels, we are surrounded by massive amounts of data, whether we talk about nutritional labels on food products or departmental KPIs on a dashboard. Discussions on data visualization have rapidly increased over the last years as more executives, managers and analysts strive for a better understanding of the raw data behind everyday dashboards, scorecards or presidential poll results, for example. The struggle is to bring the raw data to life in a simple and comprehensible manner. However, as it lacks an overview, you can perceive statistical data as overwhelming, time consuming and difficult to understand.

We use data visualization to fulfil a basic human need, that of telling a story in a more than verbal manner. Data visualization is the graphical representation of information with the purpose of communicating without words, increasing the speed at which data is comprehended by others and providing aid in the decision making process.

Communicating visually

Data visualization is not something new. Communicating data and information with visual means has been around in various forms for hundreds and arguably thousands of years. Graphical interaction with data has known a steep increasing trend among the full spectrum of users. From executives to front line personnel, data visualization is becoming a necessity. Among corporations across the globe, the line, bar, and pie charts are some of the most commonly used types of graphs. Yet, there is more to it. Today, through graphical displays of data, such as dashboards and scorecards, users are moving on from static reporting and data tables to a more interactive workspace, which allows them to better comprehend and manipulate data, as well as to reach a strategic decision by viewing past, present and future trends.

In accordance with FusionCharts' white paper on Principles of Data Visualization, in the business environment, data visualization follows two broad goals: explanatory and exploratory. In the first case, the viewer is directed along a defined path: he starts by having a question in mind and, after visualizing the data, he finds the answer. Therefore, the data tells the viewer a story. An exploratory visualization offers the viewer many dimensions to a data set, or benchmarks multiple data sets. Therefore, the viewer requires time to first familiarize himself with the visual aspect, identify an area of interest, and then explore the different dimensions of the image. Thus, the viewer finds the story that data is transmitting.

How visuals aid information retention

It has been proven that information retention after a meeting, for example, can be boosted up to six times when that information is presented through visual and oral means, instead of merely spoken words.

When processing visual information, there are two types of memory that play an important role:

> Long-Term memory (a vast store of knowledge and a record of prior events);
> Working memory (temporary background memory for an episodic buffer).

When using the long-term memory, one expects to see the information on a visualization on X and Y axes with the corresponding unit markers, or the legend graph besides it. This type of memory is formed in time by past interactions and experiences with other visualizations.

All in all, you rely on your working memory to retain the partial results while solving an arithmetic problem without paper or when noticing a number of interest on a dashboard. This type of memory breaks the vast visual information into smaller pieces, which are much easier to remember.

On the importance of effective process based visualization

Good data visualization is critical to making smarter business decisions, and it might contribute to improving performance. The need to make sense of and communicate data to others is rapidly increasing and, thus, as time passes, new ways are created to better and more efficiently deliver information in a non-verbal matter. Information technology, software and design, combined with the principles of visualization create sophisticated images and animations to aid large data sets comprehension. By covering a growing range of areas, industries and projects, visualization tools reflect creative ways of communicating data to others, with virtually no limit to what kind of information can be translated into an image. Vision is the main key to communicating information.

The data visualization process should rely on identifying the purpose of the data. The question of "what is the story of the data?" should be asked both before creating a visualization and using it.

On the other hand, sometimes it may be difficult to identify the message of a visual representation. This situation might be caused by the failure to consider best

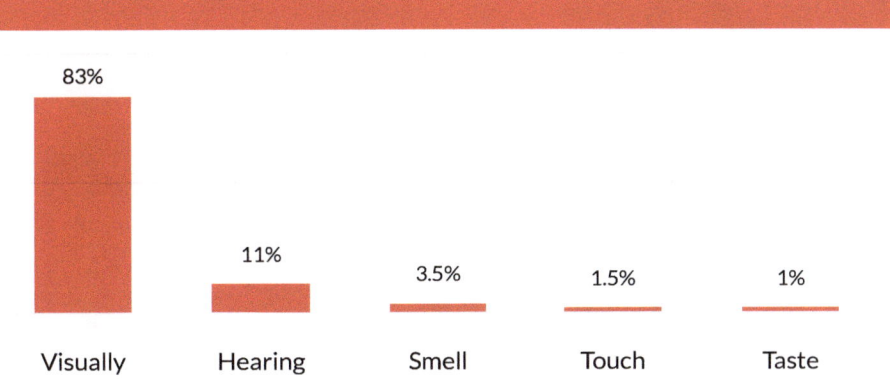

practices, such as understanding the data type, identifying the relationship between the data, keeping it simple and wasting no pixels.

Some of the benefits of efficient data visualization are:

> Action – it supports the decision making process;
> Immediacy – it provides immediate answers to the business questions that might appear, as patterns, trends and connections between variables can easily be spotted;
> Challenge – it stimulates the brain to come up with ideas. In other words, visual representations can "light the bulb";
> Insights – it draws out insights from large amounts of data.

About the pitfalls or how visuals can misinform

Visualization is becoming vital for transmitting information in a non-verbal manner, but when done wrong, it creates more confusion and ambiguity rather than provide the desired answers. Visualization ideas, which at first might seem brilliant, can turn out to be puzzling for viewers, diminishing their willingness to look for answers due to the complexity or bad representation of the data.

One of the easiest ways to misrepresent data in a visual rendition is by messing with the X and Y axis on charts, rearranging elements such as bar graphs, line graphs, or scattered plots. In most cases, the Y-axis should have a range starting from 0 to a maximum that encompasses the data range. Unfortunately, taken to an extreme, as in the example below, this technique can create a distorted view of the data, making the differences between values appear much larger than they really are. The two graphs below present the same data from two

different points of view. In the first case, it gives the impression that the interest rates have skyrocketed, while in the second case the difference is slightly observable. The difference between the lowest value and the highest value is 0.014%.

By displaying the data with a zero-baseline Y-axis, the viewer has a more realistic picture of the facts, perceiving that the rates are almost static. Such examples are widely seen almost everywhere and the question on everyone's mind is "Why start at 2.14%? Why not any other value?"

Before creating any visualization and thinking of its design, you should consider some key aspects and try to answer some of the following questions: What story will the data tell? What questions should the visualization bring forth? Which data needs to be highlighted? What is the best architecture for revealing the most important aspects of the visual? Who are the viewers?

As you answer some of these questions, the right design and implementation process can begin. It does not mean that the visual aspect will not require any changes along the way, but taking the right route in the design phase will simplify the work and help create a better and more understandable representation.

Visualizations rely on accurate and coordinated data, so it is essential to double check the data upon which the visualization is created. If the data is incomplete or faulty, or the data sets differ in definition or units, the final visualization may lead to a poor interpretation of the results, causing a faulty or misleading conclusion. Even if the data is consistent, a poorly conceived visualization might show nothing or highlight irrelevant facts. It all comes down to quality. P

BENCHMARKING:
A story of best practices and success

■ **ANDRADA-IULIA GHEȚE**

All businesses are in a continuous search for processes and quality improvements that will eventually lead them to achieving a superior level of performance in their activity.

Benchmarking represents a very important methodology, used to support significant business improvements, although it has not been, so far, explored to its full potential. Its methodological uniqueness is represented by the identification of those processes that lead to a superior performance, followed by the analysis of the facts behind that success.

What is benchmarking?

An operational definition of benchmarking, as developed by specialists in the field, is finding and implementing best practices. In regards to other definitions of benchmarking, we can refer to the Australian Manufacturing Council (AMC 1994), which defined benchmarking as „the ongoing, systematic process to search for and introduce international best practice into an organization", or to Spendolini (1992), who described benchmarking as being "the continuous and systematic process of identifying, analyzing, and adapting industries' best practices that will lead an organization to superior performance". In a nutshell, benchmarking seeks to improve one's business through the comparison of performance metrics with representative companies, from the same or different industries, which will spark innovative ideas and lead to developing superior procedures.

Benchmarking history

The term "benchmarking" has its origin in the 1970s, when it was first used for identifying a reference point from which other measurements can be made - a "benchmark". Historically, benchmarking is based on tools like the competitive advantage analysis and the Kaizen framework, which stipulate continuous incremental improvement, or "change for the best".

In the 1980s, several corporations, especially from the technological field, started introducing benchmarking as a standard organizational procedure. Prior to this, Xerox, which was the biggest copy machines manufacturer worldwide, implemented competitive benchmarking around the mid-1970's, when the company went through complete revival. Xerox compared itself directly with the best competitors in the market in order to determine what would be the best approach to increasing productivity, while decreasing costs.

Rank Xerox reworked business thinking through the benchmarking plan they have introduced. Robert C. Camp, Manager of Benchmarking Competency Quality and Customer Satisfaction at Xerox,

developed a five-phase benchmarking process, containing twelve main steps to be followed. Xerox soon became a world-class organization and the first company to win the Malcolm Baldrige National Quality Award, in 1989 and the European Quality Award in 1992.

Benchmarking benefits

A benchmarking study provides several benefits, including a set of measures for assessing the performance of the project system and a baseline for measuring improvements. It also offers the opportunity to compare an organization's performance against industry competitors, noting strengths, weaknesses, and different ways of executing projects.

Moreover, through benchmarking, companies can elaborate proposals for improving the project system, monitor organizational performance and see which of their competitors perform at the highest and lowest levels.

> **A benchmark is generally used for improving the organization's processes, communication or for budgetary reasons.**

Benchmarking process

The benchmarking process can be conducted in several ways. One option is to use benchmarking data taken from processes commonly used within an industry, or functional benchmarking data for various processes that exist in several industries. Another approach is related to internal benchmarking, that compares common activities across different divisions of the same organization.

The benchmarking process follows four main stages:
> Planning: setting objectives, literature research, stakeholders' targeting, developing the preliminary questionnaire;
> Data collection: surveys, site visits, interviews;
> Analyses: comparative statistical and practical analyses of the participating organizations, discrepancies analysis;
> Improvement: applying potential changes, resulted from studying the organization's management system, in order to improve performance, monitor progress and plan ongoing benchmarking activities.

Benchmarking types

Benchmarking can be divided into two

main categories: informal and formal benchmarking.
> *Informal benchmarking* refers to learning from others' experiences. This implies consulting with experts, networking, and obtain data from websites, online databases, or publications.
> *Formal benchmarking* can also be divided into two main categories: performance benchmarking and best practices benchmarking.

Performance benchmarking enables a performance gap to be identified and refers to the comparison of performance data obtained through studying similar processes or activities. This type of benchmarking can be conducted through comparison of financial measures or comparison of non-financial measures.

Best practice benchmarking focuses on comparing performance data obtained by studying similar processes or activities and identifying, adapting and implementing the practices that produced the best performance results. It represents the most powerful type of benchmarking, which focuses on "action" and is used for learning from the experience of others and achieving significant improvements in performance. Best practice benchmarking can also be divided into four different types, as follows: internal benchmarking, competitive benchmarking, strategic benchmarking and generic benchmarking.

Benchmarking is nowadays acknowledged as being a core component of the quality improvement methodology and can be considered one the most important contribution to it after Deming's or Juran's foundations. Deming introduced the 14 Points on Quality Management as a basis for implementing the total quality management for helping organizations increase their productivity and processes quality, whereas Juran's contributions to quality management might have been even greater, as he focused on the management's responsibility in achieving quality and the need for setting goals.

A benchmark is generally used for improving the organization's processes, communication or for budgetary reasons. Benchmarking plays a key role in helping organizations monitor their performance and deal with the policy process within their industry.

Among the factors that can determine a successful benchmarking process, the following can be mentioned: a good selection of variables to be measured, full comparison compatibility of the measured processes and a good allotment of resources. P

Q: What techniques can be used to select KPIs?

Selecting Key Performance Indicators (KPIs) is, by far, the most challenging aspect of establishing a performance management framework.

There are some techniques that can be used to facilitate the selection process:
1. KPI expo: it consists of presenting a list of KPIs during the KPI selection workshop, in order to offer participants an overview of the KPIs and to start the process keeping in mind the final outcomes.
2. KPI wall clustering: it is an exercise used to group KPIs based on objectives or relevant activities. Keep in mind that it is important to ensure interactivity between workshop participants during the exercise. Discussing each KPI and deciding on appropriate clustering ensures involvement and helps the buy-in process.
3. KPI selection criteria: it refers to defining clear specifications that will help to filter all the brainstormed KPI examples. A variety of criteria can be established, but it is important to keep the process simple and avoid using a vast array of complex filtering features.

Three basic characteristics need to be taken into consideration. KPIs should be:
> Relevant – The KPI represents a measurable expression for the achievement of a desired level of results in an area significant to the organization. It can be the achievement of a strategic objective or an aspect that is essential for decision making;
> Clearly defined – KPIs should be described by using clear and intelligible terms. It is recommended to avoid management jargons or abstract concepts;
> Balanced – Ideally, when selecting KPIs, two indicators are recommended to be monitored for each objective in order to avoid negative behavior. The risk of attaining the target for one performance indicator, while ignoring the achievement of the other can be reduced if KPIs are balanced.

Q: Why should we use KPI documentation forms?

The KPI documentation form is a template that structures the most relevant information regarding a given indicator. Some important fields of the form are the KPI definition, the calculation formula and the target. In addition, other relevant fields can be used, such as: subordinate measures, limitations and notes.

Some of the main reasons for using KPI documentation forms can be structured as follows:
> They assist in the documentation of KPIs in a clear,

> *The process of strategic planning must be continuously reviewed on year term basis and the link with Performance Management is the key*
>
> Maria Elena Sanz Ibarra, HR Director, Ministry of Transportation and Telecommunications, Chile

structured and standardized manner;
> They provide detailed information about each indicator;
> They ensure consistency in measuring and interpreting KPIs;
> They enhance KPIs understanding.

The most important functions of the KPI documentation forms are:
> Communication facilitator through standardization;
> Automation enabler;
> Knowledge management facilitator;
> Stakeholders' educator (KPI owners and data custodians);
> Buy-in enabler, by involving stakeholders.

Q: How can KPIs be activated?

Activating KPIs is an important challenge that companies face after implementing a performance management system.

What techniques can be used to make sure that KPIs are activated?
> Meeting KPI data custodians in person;
> Involving data custodians in a community of practice;
> Sending reminder emails.
Meeting KPI data custodians in person brings three main benefits:
> It captures attention, especially when new initiatives or projects are developed;
> It inspires a positive emotional atmosphere that paves the way for innovation and collaboration;
> It builds human networks and business relationships.

Involving data custodians in a community of practice translates into promoting the importance of exploring and communicating current and best practices in working with data for KPIs. The technique offers three main advantages:
> It provides a common platform for data custodians to

communicate and share work related experience;

> It stimulates learning by supplying a medium for sharing best practices and tutoring;

> It creates collaborative processes that add value and maximize data custodian efficiency.

Sending reminder emails is another KPI activation technique that can be used. It may seem very straight forward, but many companies underestimate the importance and efficiency of this technique. Sending reminder emails creates a sense of urgency in regards to the data gathering process and serves as a notice for data custodians that are not on schedule with providing data.

Q: Which are the challenges in setting targets?

A target reflects the desired level of a Key Performance Indicator (KPI). Targets make the results derived from measurement more meaningful and provide organizations with feedback regarding performance. They are a mandatory prerequisite for each KPI measured, and should be quantifiable and clearly expressed.

The process of setting targets should be based on sound research. Sources of relevant information are: internal historical data, benchmarking reports and, in some instances, even annual reports from competitors or other companies from the same or a similar industry.

Setting the right targets is, in most cases, an adjustment process. Acknowledging the internal capabilities of the company is essential, but testing different target levels can lead to experiential learning and eventually to the right target.

Some examples of challenges that can appear when using targets are:

> Keeping targets ambitious, yet attainable;

> Preventing negative behaviors that may occur by overemphasizing reaching targets;

> Maintaining flexibility and adjusting targets.

> *Many organizations will give up before they actually start to get the results. It's about these two things: know what you want and be disciplined in applying the tools to get it!*
>
> Gregory Richards, Professor of Performance Management, Telfer School of Management, University of Ottawa, Canada

Establishing targets is just the first step towards high performance, as adjustments to the internal processes and constant analyses on obtained results, compared to fixed marks, are necessary to achieve the desired performance, in a healthy manner.

Q: Which are the key steps to implementing an Individual Performance Management System?

Individual performance management systems, which offer employees and managers an opportunity to identify strengths and weaknesses in their performance and establish new directions for improvement, imply following 6 key steps in order be properly implemented.

> **Step #1** Clarify the organizational context: This refers to reviewing the organization's current state and its needs, which require the implementation of an individual performance management system. It helps not only in understanding the organizational culture and employee perceptions regarding such a system, but also in identifying the obstacles that might influence a successful implementation.

> **Step #2** Establish the system implementation project plan: It refers to following all the necessary steps for implementing the performance management system at individual level (i.e. obtaining project approval, designing the project implementation plan, project communication to stakeholders, project initiation, monitoring and continuous review).

> **Step #3** Define components and templates used: It can be done by analyzing best case practices or through the HR manager's recommendations. Managers need to establish standardized templates that will therefore be used within their organizations.

> **Step #4** Presentations and training sessions for management and employees: They should be implemented in order to ensure that both the management and the employees understand the individual performance management system and the project implementation plan. During these sessions, the purpose and objectives of using such a system will be explained, along with the role assigned to each employee.

> **Step #5** Project implementation: It refers to the start-up phase of the system implementation, by using all components. It implies stakeholder involvement and system validation during the process, for continuous improvement.

> **Step #6** System monitoring and review: The purpose of this step is comparing current results with the expected ones and analyzing the outcomes. System monitoring and continuous reviews will help in achieving the project's objectives in due time.

CRISTINA TĂRÂȚĂ
Head of Research Programs, The KPI Institute

MIHAI TOMA
Head of Professional Practice TKI MENA

ANDREEA VECERDEA
Head Of Performance Management Office Sibiu, The KPI Institute

RAMONA GLIGOREA
Talent Development Specialist, The KPI Institute

LIFESTYLE

NUTRITION 2.0
Eat. Track. Perform.

▌ ADELINA CHELNICIUC

Nutrition trends

In 2014, many trends that hesitantly appeared over the last few years are being revitalized. From different types of diets and food trends, to using numerous types of gadgets meant for measuring one's health and fitness level.

The Dairy Council of California has recently released their Top 10 Nutrition Trends for 2014, which offers details about the current food and nutrition issues. The trends they have identified are also completed by the Food Technology magazine and New Nutrition Business. Some of the main trends of this year, which identify the most impacting changes in the way people choose to eat, buy and consequently behave and feel are:

1. **Natural food:** the main focus is on giving up on the so-called "junk food" and turning towards natural, fresh food grows, such as gluten-free or low sodium products. The trend applies both to producers and consumers. Let's take, for example, the nutrition labels. Consumers seem to have an insatiable appetite for nutrition and diet information, as they got used to reading the labels, and more and more people now count their daily number of calories or even choose products based on information from food labels, while producers provide this piece of information even when not mandatory, proving their customers transparency and interest for their physical well-being. Millennials, quoted by Forbes in their article Consumers Not Lovin' Fast Food As Much These Days, has recently reported a 20% decrease in visits to fast food chains, showing an obvious increase in people's concern for their health and physical well-being, in the detriment of saving money or time;

2. **The extensive use of proteins:** in the last couple of years, proteins have been increasingly acknowledged for their multiple benefits when it comes to health and fitness, escalating to the point where they have become one of the main assets in weight management and muscle building;

3. **The so-called "performance nutrition":** far from targeting professional athletes only, nutrition bars, energy drinks and other similar products are now used by a large amount of people, regardless of their involvement in sports, be it casual jogging or a simple recreational activity.

More and more people are now taking healthy living to a whole new level, by fully understanding the importance of nutrition and acting accordingly. Monitoring one's daily diet is no longer regarded as a matter of losing weight, or as exhaustively attached to the fashion industry. It is, on the contrary, understood for its real value, as a means of control and awareness.

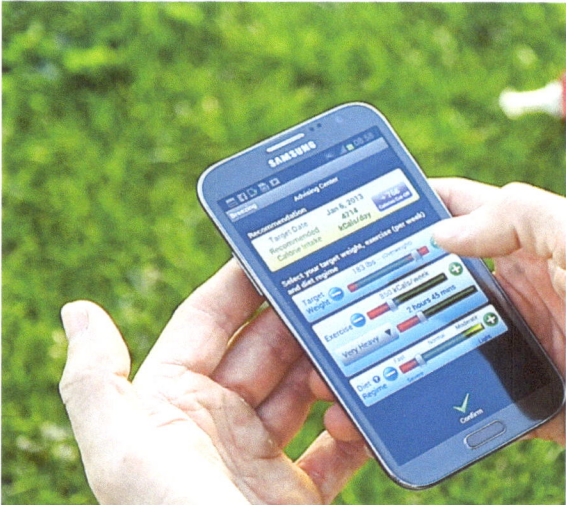

Tracking trends

The fact that people tend to adopt new and improved nutrition habits is now becoming clear. In this context, the need to have better clarity and focus on their habits and results comes naturally. These are the reasons why many people have turned towards using different gadgets to measure their daily activities.

When it comes to nutrition, there are many tools that people can use in order to count their calories and even plan their diet, from simple mobile phone apps to wearable monitors, that keep track of the calories burned or steps taken throughout the day, in addition to other aspects, such as heart rate or sleep quality. Some of these gadgets even allow people to establish their own targets, as it is well known that setting clear goals boosts one's motivation to take actions in order to achieve them.

What do all these trends tell us? Are people becoming too self-centered, too obsessed with their physical appearance, too superficial? Not at all. This issue has to be regarded from a totally different perspective. Physical well-being strongly influences one's psychological state, in aspects such as self-confidence, memory, mood, or even one's ability to concentrate. All this eventually translates into performance, both in personal life and at work.

MIHAI PĂCULEA

Samsung Gear S
complete mobility

Samsung Gear S is a fitness companion that allows you to monitor your health, featuring enhanced multi sensors and a built in GPS. It is designed to coach and help motivate people that are using it during fitness programs. It also includes some features that are not fitness-related, like the S Voice, that literally takes tasks off your hands, and the 24-hour News Briefing that offers the most attractive news during the past 24 hours.

Dash Smart Headphones
it's all in your head

Dash Smart Headphones are the world's first wireless smart in-ear headphones that allow you to play, track and talk. The Dash tracks movement, like pace, steps, cadence and distance and provides an overview of your personal performance during a full day or a fitness session. It can also memorize users' goals to produce an overview of the performance milestones that have been met according to the established goals. All this feedback is provided in real time, in an acoustic way through headphones. The most brilliant feature is that it even works without an attached smartphone. Effectively, they are the single smallest and most complex personal performance tracking tool, with communications on top.

A new era dawns on our personal life, as our environment is slowly but certainly embracing technology. Devices, gadgets, apps and appliances are all being assimilated in routine activities, adding a new dimension to one's daily experience. Although a lot of these new devices are labeled as being created for leisure and daily assistance, all of them can be used to measure performance in our personal life and to track the evolution towards the milestones we establish for ourselves.

Google Lens
feast your eyes

Google developers are not only making computers wearable and cars driverless – They are also using their expertise to help healthcare develop, by building a gadget with which diabetics can keep track of their sugar level.

The contact lens uses processors, a glucose sensor that has been specially developed for the Google Lens and an antenna, thinner than a human hair that communicates the results to a device, like a smartphone. What will the process look like? The sensor detects glucose levels in the wearer's tears, collecting readings once every second, which are transmitted by an antenna to an external device. This device could greatly increase the quality of life for diabetics, who have to monitor their blood sugar levels throughout the day.

Nod Ring
one ring to rule them all

Its main purpose is to transform movements into commands for the technological devices around us such as: laptops, Smart TVs, and some ambient features. It sums up a number of advantages and wraps them all around your little finger. It can be used for professional purposes, for example during a presentation, to swipe slides, to start/stop it; or everyday activities, like changing channels on your TVs, or typing notes without even touching anything. One of its neatest features is that with this ring, graphic designers can improve their performance because they are using their hands not a mouse or any other device to create pictures and designs. And these are just a few of the Nod Rings' features.

TOP 25 KPIS REPORTS

- Extensive collections of the most visited KPIs on smartkpis.com, across functional areas and industries;

- Thorough analysis of each KPI according to smartKPIs.com documentation form and standards;

- Proof-of-concept of relevant KPIs, documented at best practice standards.

Explore the extensive Top KPIs series dedicated to analyzing the most popular KPIs by visiting:
http://store.kpiinstitute.org/publications.html

Best-selling Top KPIs Reports

Reports by Functional Area

 Top 25 Application Development KPIs of 2011-2012

 Top 25 Contract Management KPIs of 2011-2012

 Top 25 Customer Service KPIs of 2011-2012

 Top 25 Data Center KPIs of 2011-2012

Top 25 Enterprise Architecture KPIs of 2011-2012

 Top 25 Human Resources KPIs of 2011-2012

 Top 25 Information Technology KPIs of 2011-2012

Top 25 Innovation KPIs of 2011-2012

Top 25 IT Security KPIs of 2011-2012

 Top 25 Portfolio Management KPIs of 2011-2012

Top 25 Procurement / Purchasing KPIs of 2011-2012

Top 25 Production KPIs of 2011-2012

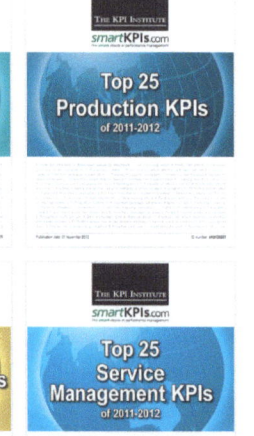 Top 25 Project Management KPIs of 2011-2012

Top 25 Risk Management KPIs of 2011-2012

Top 25 Service Management KPIs of 2011-2012

Reports by Industry

 Top 25 Academic Education KPIs of 2011-2012

 Top 25 Airlines KPIs of 2011-2012

 Top 25 Airports KPIs of 2011-2012

 Top 25 Banking and Credit KPIs of 2011-2012

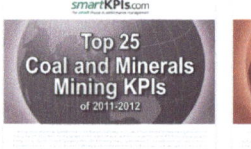 Top 25 Coal and Minerals Mining KPIs of 2011-2012

 Top 25 Healthcare KPIs of 2011-2012

 Top 25 Hospitals KPIs of 2011-2012

 Top 25 Hotel KPIs of 2011-2012

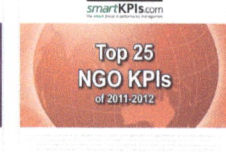 Top 25 NGO KPIs of 2011-2012

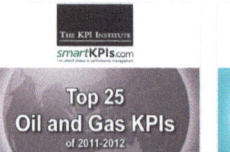 Top 25 Oil and Gas KPIs of 2011-2012

 Top 25 Ports KPIs of 2011-2012

 Top 25 Restaurant KPIs of 2011-2012

 Top 25 Retail KPIs of 2011-2012

Top 25 Shipping KPIs of 2011-2012

 Top 25 Telecommunications KPIs of 2011-2012

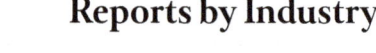

Reports by Functional Area

Top 25 Accounting KPIs of 2013-2015
Top 25 Accounts Payable and Receivable KPIs of 2013-2015
Top 25 Administration / Office Support KPIs of 2013-2015
Top 25 Advertising KPIs of 2013-2015
Top 25 Application Development KPIs of 2013-2015
Top 25 Asset Management KPIs of 2013-2015
Top 25 Compensation and Benefits KPIs of 2013-2015
Top 25 Compliance and Audit Management KPIs of 2013-2015
Top 25 Contract Management KPIs of 2013-2015
Top 25 Corporate Travel KPIs of 2013-2015
Top 25 CSR KPIs of 2013-2015
Top 25 Customer Service KPIs of 2013-2015
Top 25 Data Center KPIs of 2013-2015
Top 25 eCommerce KPIs of 2013-2015
Top 25 Efficiency and Effectiveness KPIs of 2013-2015
Top 25 Email Marketing KPIs of 2013-2015
Top 25 Enterprise Architecture KPIs of 2013-2015
Top 25 Environmental Care KPIs of 2013-2015
Top 25 Facilities Management KPIs of 2013-2015
Top 25 Finance KPIs of 2013-2015
Top 25 Forecasts & Valuation KPIs of 2013-2015
Top 25 Governance KPIs of 2013-2015
Top 25 HSSE KPIs of 2013-2015
Top 25 Human Resources KPIs of 2013-2015
Top 25 Information Technology KPIs of 2013-2015
Top 25 Innovation KPIs of 2013-2015
Top 25 Inventory Management KPIs of 2013-2015
Top 25 IT Security KPIs of 2013-2015
Top 25 Knowledge Management KPIs of 2013-2015
Top 25 Legal Services KPIs of 2013-2015

Top 25 Liquidity KPIs of 2013-2015
Top 25 Logistics / Distribution KPIs of 2013-2015
Top 25 Maintenance KPIs of 2013-2015
Top 25 Management KPIs of 2013-2015
Top 25 Marketing KPIs of 2013-2015
Top 25 Network Management KPIs of 2013-2015
Top 25 Online Advertising KPIs of 2013-2015
Top 25 Online Publishing - Weblogs KPIs of 2013-2015
Top 25 Portfolio Management KPIs of 2013-2015
Top 25 Procurement / Purchasing KPIs of 2013-2015
Top 25 Production KPIs of 2013-2015
Top 25 Profitability KPIs of 2013-2015
Top 25 Project Management KPIs of 2013-2015
Top 25 Public Relations KPIs of 2013-2015
Top 25 Quality Management KPIs of 2013-2015
Top 25 R&D KPIs of 2013-2015
Top 25 Recruitment KPIs of 2013-2015
Top 25 Retention KPIs of 2013-2015
Top 25 Risk Management KPIs of 2013-2015
Top 25 Sales KPIs of 2013-2015*
Top 25 Search Engine Optimisation (SEO) KPIs of 2013-2015
Top 25 Service Delivery KPIs of 2013-2015
Top 25 Service Management KPIs of 2013-2015
Top 25 Supply Chain Management KPIs of 2013-2015
Top 25 Supply Chain*, Procurement, Distribution KPIs of 2013-2015
Top 25 Talent Development KPIs of 2013-2015
Top 25 Web Analytics KPIs of 2013-2015
Top 25 Workforce KPIs of 2013-2015
Top 25 Working Environment KPIs of 2013-2015

Reports by Industry

Top 25 Academic Education KPIs of 2013-2015
Top 25 Accounting Services KPIs of 2013-2015
Top 25 Airlines KPIs of 2013-2015
Top 25 Airports KPIs of 2013-2015
Top 25 Banking and Credit KPIs of 2013-2015
Top 25 Broadcasting (TV and Radio) KPIs of 2013-2015
Top 25 Business Consulting KPIs of 2013-2015
Top 25 Call Center KPIs of 2013-2015
Top 25 Civil Engineering KPIs of 2013-2015
Top 25 Coaching / Training KPIs of 2013-2015
Top 25 Coal and Minerals Mining KPIs of 2013-2015
Top 25 Colleges and Universities KPIs of 2013-2015
Top 25 Construction of Buildings KPIs of 2013-2015
Top 25 Crops KPIs of 2013-2015
Top 25 Customs KPIs of 2013-2015
Top 25 Electricity KPIs of 2013-2015
Top 25 Emergency Response / Ambulance Services KPIs of 2013-2015
Top 25 Engineering KPIs of 2013-2015
Top 25 Event Production and Promotion KPIs of 2013-2015
Top 25 Film and Music KPIs of 2013-2015
Top 25 Forestry and Logging KPIs of 2013-2015
Top 25 Healthcare KPIs of 2013-2015
Top 25 Hospitals KPIs of 2013-2015
Top 25 Hotel KPIs of 2013-2015
Top 25 Insurance KPIs of 2013-2015
Top 25 Investments KPIs of 2013-2015
Top 25 Land Transport (Road & Rail) KPIs of 2013-2015
Top 25 Legal Practice KPIs of 2013-2015
Top 25 Libraries and Archives KPIs of 2013-2015
Top 25 Livestock, Hunting and Fishing KPIs of 2013-2015
Top 25 Local Government KPIs of 2013-2015
Top 25 Local Public Transport KPIs of 2013-2015

Top 25 Medical Laboratory KPIs of 2013-2015
Top 25 Medical Practice KPIs of 2013-2015
Top 25 Mortgages KPIs of 2013-2015
Top 25 Museums KPIs of 2013-2015
Top 25 Natural Gas KPIs of 2013-2015
Top 25 NGO KPIs of 2013-2015
Top 25 Oil and Gas KPIs of 2013-2015
Top 25 Pension Funds KPIs of 2013-2015
Top 25 Ports KPIs of 2013-2015
Top 25 Postal and Courier Services KPIs of 2013-2015
Top 25 Preventive Healthcare KPIs of 2013-2015
Top 25 Primary and Secondary Schools / K-12 KPIs of 2013-2015
Top 25 Property Management KPIs of 2013-2015
Top 25 Publishing KPIs of 2013-2015
Top 25 Railways KPIs of 2013-2015
Top 25 Real Estate Development KPIs of 2013-2015
Top 25 Real Estate Transactions KPIs of 2013-2015
Top 25 Recruitment / Employment Activities KPIs of 2013-2015
Top 25 Restaurant KPIs of 2013-2015
Top 25 Retail KPIs of 2013-2015
Top 25 Roads KPIs of 2013-2015
Top 25 Shipping KPIs of 2013-2015
Top 25 Social Media KPIs of 2013-2015
Top 25 Sport Club Management KPIs of 2013-2015
Top 25 Sport Event Organisation KPIs of 2013-2015
Top 25 State Government KPIs of 2013-2015
Top 25 Sustainability KPIs of 2013-2015
Top 25 Telecommunications KPIs of 2013-2015
Top 25 Tour Operator KPIs of 2013-2015
Top 25 Training and Other Education KPIs of 2013-2015
Top 25 Travel Agency KPIs of 2013-2015
Top 25 Water and Sewage KPIs of 2013-2015

SOFTWARE REVIEW

▌ MIHAI PĂCULEA

What are the trends in Data Analytics?

First of all, we need to understand that this field witnesses continuous adjustments and developments. Decisive changes are happening in the world of Business Intelligence (BI) and Analytics, which include data discovery techniques, real-time data analysis and better in-depth analysis of mature data.

Why is it happening?

In the past few years, there has been a continuous drop in costs for data acquiring, storing and managing. Consequently, more and more companies find it practical and cost-efficient to apply BI and Analytics in a lot of situations, in order to minimize the risk of taking a bad decision.

So, where are we now in Data Analytics?

Consistent with this behavioral change among managers and corporations, BI platforms now switch to more user-friendly and analysis-centric solutions. To be able to create an analysis-centric solution that would be used by large amounts of people, the BI software platforms are now adopting more accessible interfaces, based on many drag and drop options and abounding in alternatives for customizing the way data analysis is generated.

Another factor that influences the evolution of software products over the next years is clouding. The cost of clouding information is dropping very fast and its well known advantages (high-security level and backed-up information) are catching the attention of BI managers', who start investing in the development of such solutions. From a user's point of view, the biggest advantage is the possibility to access this information from anywhere, using any laptop, without being tied to the work station.

This increases managers' flexibility and, therefore, the flexibility of the entire decision making process.

And yet, there is more in terms of increasing the portability of software solutions. Today, most of top BI solutions are integrating their software solutions on platforms such as Android and iOS, as lots of managers demand to have the data available at any moment of the day, naturally integrated within their activities.

What's in store for Data Analytics?

After most of small to medium companies will have embraced these Data Analytics trends, and large companies will have gotten familiar with gathering data and implementing it in a BI solution, it's time for the next step in achieving organizational performance. This step will be represented by predictive analytics, which encompass a variety of statistical techniques from modeling, machine learning and data mining, along with analyzing current and historical data in order to make predictions about future events or future behavioral patterns.

The most common types of predictive analytics are predictive models, descriptive models and decision models. Most managers are interested in the latter ones, in order to better understand the potential results and impact behind decisions and to lower the probability of failure caused by taking a non-fact based decision.

Another very challenging aspect is finding a way to use unstructured information. There is a lot of unstructured information that is now ignored by business managers due to the time needed to structure and transform it into data that is useful for the decision making process. This will only happen if NoSQL technologies will improve the way this information is structured into data, as well as the analyzing options they provide for the final user.

Here are some examples of software products that best illustrate the above mentioned trends:

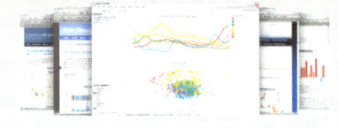

Tableau Software: it benefits from a highly intuitive, visual-based data discovery. Its dashboarding and data mashup capabilities met business users' expectations about what they can discover in data and sharing possibilities, without extensive BI platforms skills or training;

Qlikview: one of the main reason Qlik became a market leader is because of its capabilities in data discovery;

IBM Software Solutions: IBM offers a complete range of enterprise-grade BI, performance management and advanced analytics platform capabilities;

Tibco: is known as one of the early leaders in the field of data discovery, with a flexible, easy-to-use platform for user-driven information, exploration and analysis. Another important and very strong advantage is the capability of publishing interactive and visual dashboards, building predictive models and producing analytic applications.

Reading for performance

■ DENISA CĂLIN

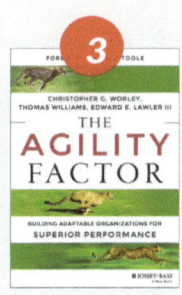
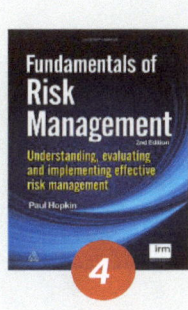

Armstrong's Handbook of Performance Management: An Evidence-Based Guide to Delivering High Performance

by Michael Armstrong

This addition to the Performance Management literature represents the latest version of Michael Armstorng's series of handbooks. This edition brings new light to this classical text by including the most recent developments in managing individual performance for driving business growth and comes with useful tools and management practice data from more than 150 organizations.

Performance Management in Nonprofit Organizations: Global Perspectives

by Zahirul Hoque (Editor), Lee Parker (Editor)

Moving to prove that performance management is about more than money, this book represents a research-based resource for academics, students and practitioners alike. Inspired from the reality of today's non-profit and non-governmental organizations, which prompts for accountability and transparency, the book focuses on current issues, designing and implementing performance management systems and performance management measurements for this very particular sector.

The Agility Factor: Building Adaptable Organizations for Superior Performance

by Christopher G. Worley, Thomas D. Williams and Edward E. Lawler III

This books dives into the topic of building long-term business profitability, uncovering what factors drive and guarantee profitability in the long run. The material is the result of a massive study, conducted on over 200 large companies, which highlight agility as the main agent for sustainable and, yes, highly profitable long-term business endeavors. Ample examples are provided, in the form of case studies, for helping managers across industries turn their companies into highly successful businesses.

Fundamentals of Risk Management: Understanding, Evaluating and Implementing Effective Risk Management

by Paul Hopkin

Launched recently, the book brings fresh knowledge on how to take on organizational risk. Bringing extensive descriptions, in international case studies and examples from both the private and public sectors, the book brings practical insights for assessing and managing organizational risk, with implications for improving a company's performance and resilience.

Arts Governance: People, Passion, Performance

by Ruth Rentschler

Saluting the emergent enterprising arts organizations, the book brings about the importance of performance management in a cultural context. Based on actual research, that drafts on employing numerous research methodologies and a large number of data from the field, the book brings an innovative answer to impending issues affiliated to managing and operating an arts organizations.

The Marketing Performance Blueprint: Strategies and Technologies to Build and Measure Business Success

by Paul Roetzer

This new addition to the performance literature moves to prove what can happen when science and marketing mastery work for and with your organization. All with a keen focus on processes, tools, technology and strategies for helping performance-driven organizations attain their performance goals.

RECOMMENDED

THE HUMAN SCALE

■ MIHAI TOMA

The Human Scale, a documentary directed by Andreas Møl Dalsgaard, tackles a problematic issue in today's social environment. At the moment, 50% of the world's population lives in urban areas, but by 2050 this is assumed to increase to 80%. The end result will be a greater growing rate of megalopolises.

Currently, cities are being planned with an emphasis on highway or freeway systems, high-rise buildings and work spaces. This approach has led to material gains, but the costs in human interaction, happiness and social life have not been measured, and the consequences are noticeable on many levels. Growing violence and insecurity. Social exclusion at an ever greater scale. Human alienation and social phobia. Depression and anxiety. These are the society's most common diseases today.

In the past 40 years, the Danish architect Jan Gehl has studied exactly this: human behavior in large cities and how the physical environment affects human beings on an emotional and social level. This has lead to studies on how human beings use the streets, how they walk, see, rest, meet, interact in a modern day city. He answered questions like: How many people pass this street throughout a 24 hour period? What is the percentage of pedestrians? How many are driving cars or bikes? How much of the street space are various groups allowed to use? Is this street performing well for all its users?

The research made by the Danish architect was based on a quantitative analysis of the pedestrian traffic in a city and how this is influenced by the city's infrastructure. His research fulminated in the planning of Denmark's capital, Copenhagen. The main idea was to put people in the center of the equation, as opposed to buildings or highway systems. Walking streets, bike paths, the reorganization of parks, squares and other public spaces have made Copenhagen the world's most livable city in 2013, according to Monocle Magazine.

The documentary portrays how cities like Melbourne, Dhaka, New York, Chongqing and Christchurch are now also being inspired by Gehl's work and by the developments in Copenhagen. The most famous example, New York, adopted this approach in 2007. Broadway, and more especially Times Square, were the focus of the city planners. They limited traffic in the area, created walking spaces, bike lanes and set up areas where people could gather to socialize and interact. The

Are people just going to wait for this future city to be built?

positive results were visible: 74% of people applauded the changes and there was a decrease in injuries by 63%. Times Square is now the most frequented place in New York, as proven by its 50 million visitors per year.

Although the documentary focuses on adopting a "human scale" in the way cities are designed, there are further ramifications that can be developed from here. In the business world, recent studies have shown that employee satisfaction and engagement, as well as customer satisfaction are crucial to the success and evolution of any company. The proper emphasis on human resources within a business is a very important performance driver.

Using a similar approach when developing business strategies and goals may be the way to the future. A business environment based on a "human scale" may be beneficial in the same way cities have benefited from it. A functional and more natural interaction between employees and management, customers and employees is one of the expected results. This will most likely lead to engaged employees and satisfied customers and, as a result, to a more productive and successful company.

www.ingramcontent.com/pod-product-compliance
Lightning Source LLC
Chambersburg PA
CBHW050757180526
45159CB00003B/1490